Making Coaching Matter

Leading Continuous Improvement in Schools

Sarah L. Woulfin
Isobel Stevenson
Kerry Lord

TEACHERS COLLEGE PRESS

TEACHERS COLLEGE | COLUMBIA UNIVERSITY
NEW YORK AND LONDON

To Toby, my tiger. And for Jeff, the feminist who ensures I thrive. —SLW

For Ken, Douglas, and Andrew. Of course. —IS

For Julian and Lucas, who continue to shape me with their love. —KHL

Published by Teachers College Press,® 1234 Amsterdam Avenue, New York, NY 10027

Library of Congress Cataloging-in-Publication Data

Names: Woulfin, Sarah, author. | Stevenson, Isobel, author. | Lord, Kerry, author.
Title: Making coaching matter : leading continuous improvement in schools / Sarah L. Woulfin, Isobel Stevenson, and Kerry Lord.
Description: New York : Teachers College Press, [2023] | Includes bibliographical references and index.
Identifiers: LCCN 2022053247 (print) | LCCN 2022053248 (ebook) | ISBN 9780807768334 (hardcover) | ISBN 9780807768327 (paperback) | ISBN 9780807781715 (ebook)
Subjects: LCSH: Mentoring in education—United States. | School improvement programs—United States. | Educational change—United States. | Educational leadership—United States.
Classification: LCC LB1731.4 .W68 2023 (print) | LCC LB1731.4 (ebook) | DDC 371.102—dc23/eng/20230104
LC record available at https://lccn.loc.gov/2022053247
LC ebook record available at https://lccn.loc.gov/2022053248

ISBN 978-0-8077-6832-7 (paper)
ISBN 978-0-8077-6833-4 (hardcover)
ISBN 978-0-8077-8171-5 (ebook)

Printed on acid-free paper
Manufactured in the United States of America

Contents

Preface

Coaching is a rapidly growing feature of the United States' educational landscape, particularly in the quest to improve the quality of teaching and learning and strengthen the leadership of principals and superintendents. Holding tandem responsibilities for supporting adult learning and promoting organizational change, coaches are lauded as leaders of professional learning. Thus, coaching has become an attractive option for improving educators' craft; how can it *not* be a good idea to hire kind and successful educators to help fellow educators get better at what they do? At the same time, there remain flaws in and misunderstandings of coaching models and activities. There also remain gaps in the infrastructure for coaching. Together, these issues contribute to coaches encountering challenges to fully achieve the vision of coaching in their context, leading to questions about the value of coaching in and for educational reform. Yet, the proliferation of coaching—across states, levels, and foci—continues. Given the considerable expense of hiring coaches, it is surprising that coaching does not come under greater scrutiny.

Acknowledging both the popularity and complexity of coaching, this book discusses how district and school leaders can increase their return on their investment in coaching. We share ideas about using coaching to advance a strategy, to construct effective coaching systems, to bridge research, theory, policy, and practice, and, ultimately, to support individual-, organizational-, and system-level improvement in service of equity and excellence. We care about formulating a vision and model for what coaching could be if leaders, teachers, and even coaches understood it better, supported it better, and built infrastructure to enable coaching for equitable improvement. Further, we seek to show how leaders and other educators might structure, enact, and promote coaching. As part of this, we present action steps to gauge, and then refine, the nature of coaching systems to align with strategy and yield improvement.

While presenting ideas on the infrastructure that makes coaching matter, we are not advocating a specific recipe for coaching. Quite the contrary, since this book explains principles and structures of coaching, discusses strengths and limitations of various approaches to coaching, and encourages analysis, reflection, and further conversations on coaching among varied educators.

In writing this book, we draw on our experiences as practitioners and researchers across multiple states and within different district contexts. Collectively, we have served as teachers, instructional coaches, leadership coaches, equity coaches, principals, central office leaders, consultants, trainers of coaches, and university professors. In these positions, we created and used observation forms and checklists, held teacher feedback meetings in classrooms, principal offices, and via Zoom, and facilitated team and large group professional development on topics ranging from phonics assessments and teacher evaluation procedures to anti-racist worldviews. We have received sparkly thank-you notes from some educators, while engaging with other educators who perceived coaching as stressful or onerous. Importantly, we have also been coached to grow—not only as teachers, leaders, and scholars but as runners, writers, cooks, and moms. This coaching has been structured and organic, in-person and online, and ongoing and haphazard. We extend gratitude to each and every coach who helped *us* find clarity and improve.

We have also engaged in research on coaching, with attention to the nature of coaches' work, principals' role in coaching, and professional development for coaches. This boundary-spanning research included collecting and analyzing data on the design and enactment of coaching to answer questions about conditions under which coaching can thrive. We detected major differences across the on-paper definitions of coaching and heard leaders' and coaches' confusion regarding what coaches should focus on, how to improve coaching, and how to enmesh coaching into the structures and culture of the building or district. Throughout, we reflected on the promise and potential of coaching to improve schools as workplaces and catalyze equitable changes for students and communities.

To be transparent, the idea for writing this book arose from feeling frustrated when seeing coaching under-utilized, under-valued, and under-leveraged. We have worked with too many coaches who feel unseen and unsupported by educational leaders who may be unfamiliar with coaching or don't know how to realize its potential, and we have worked with too many leaders who recognize that coaching has not been as effective as they desire, yet these leaders have lacked resources to help them optimize coaching. We hope administrators, coaches, and teachers read this book to develop their understanding of the intersection of coaching, strategic improvement, and equity; to gain clarity on the role of organizational conditions and leadership in influencing the nature and quality of coaching; and to gain ideas for changing structures, tools, and routines for coaching.

Education is a profoundly social endeavor, a structured response to a universal human compulsion to know more and do better. Education is also enormously complex, with more theory, research, and skills to master than any one person could possibly accomplish. Educators, therefore, must work collectively and in concert to execute all the many functions involved in educating children. Coaching is about helping educators get better at fulfilling their role in this extraordinarily complex system, and it is, therefore, challenging beyond measure.

To the extent that there is a typical coach, it is an experienced teacher who holds a reputation for success inside the classroom. In addition, coaches frequently have other traits that are part of the between-the-lines job description: reliability, conscientiousness, initiative, and compassion. Our experience of coaches is that they are not only the best teachers in the organization, they are also the best *people*. They are often exactly the people you would want on your team whatever your field, which is, frankly, why we love working with them so much.

Many coaches do not desire to be in positions of authority—otherwise they would race to become principals. But they are ambitious in other senses—on behalf of students, families, and the school community and on behalf of the mission of the organization. They generally have a very strong sense of what is right and what should be done to improve students' experiences and outcomes. And coaches can be impatient about getting the work done to produce benefits for schools. Here, we note that coaches often sense the fierce urgency of improving teaching, leadership, and learning to reach equity-oriented goals.

Above all, we have faith in the extraordinary educators who coach, engage in coaching, and lead coaches in districts across the United States and beyond. Our best professional experiences have involved working with educators who want to create stellar opportunities for all students (and adults) in their schools, and who are working to get better at getting better. We respect and admire their commitment and hope this book supports their extraordinary efforts.

LOOKING AHEAD

Our book begins by delving into coaches' on-the-ground activities and the underlying rationale for coaching as a tool for improvement. Drawing on theory, research, and practice, Chapter 1 introduces the deep-seated ideas underlying coaching and why reformers and leaders should strive to make coaching matter. Chapter 2 offers insights on high-leverage coaching routines, including how they strengthen trusting relationships and promote learning and change. Chapter 3 illuminates the history, policies, and deep-seated conceptualizations that undergird coaching.

Chapter 4 devotes attention to the intersection of coaching and equity, including how coaching can promote equity-oriented change, and how to apply an equity lens while enacting coaching routines. Within this chapter (and throughout the book), we apply National Equity Project's definition: *Educational equity means that each child receives what they need to develop to their full academic and social potential.* Further, we take the stance that equity in education involves transforming institutions and systems to disrupt the connection between a student's racial, economic, (dis)ability, cultural, or other marginalized identity, and their academic and long-term life outcomes.

In Chapter 5 of *Making Coaching Matter,* we unpack how coaching should be designed and implemented in support of strategy. We discuss how coaching can work in concert with strategy for improvement to advance coherent, equity-oriented change.

The next portion of the book addresses how to create infrastructure for strategic, equity-centered coaching. This includes building capacity for coaching and continually improving coaching as a reform lever. Chapter 6 explains how to provide professional development (PD) on coaching for educators in different roles so that coaches can engage in high-leverage activities to reach strategic, equitable goals.

Chapter 7 breaks new ground by discussing how coaching reflects tenets of continuous improvement, while simultaneously supporting continuous improvement activities within educational organizations. In this book, we define continuous improvement as cyclical, evidence-based, collaborative, reflective activities that intend to foster change (Boudett et al., 2020; Bryk et al., 2015). And, in Chapter 7, we elevate coaches' role in and for continuous improvement. The chapter also describes how leaders can evaluate the implementation of coaching to understand how strategic, equity-centered coaching is, *or is not,* occurring. In sum, this section extends the field's understanding of the infrastructure to optimize coaching.

Finally, we attend to the nuances of coaching programs, encouraging attention to similarities and differences across models and activities. Chapter 8 portrays the wide array of coaching models, highlighting differences in who is coaching whom on what, the power of those coaches, and the nature of their coaching activities. The Conclusion shares ideas on the past, present, and future of coaching, while encouraging efforts to refine structures and activities of coaching to make coaching matter, particularly in light of unprecedented issues facing the education system. While encouraging caring approaches to leadership and reform, we highlight the pressing need to make coaching matter because equitable educational improvement matters.

Throughout this book, we braid together practice, policy, and research to guide thinking, planning, and collective learning on coaching as a lever for improvement across levels of the education system. We elevate the notion that continuous improvement and ongoing learning are vital to make coaching matter and foster equity to benefit children and communities. We sincerely desire that reading, engaging with, and reflecting on this book will help district and school leaders promote coaching, so coaches, in turn, can do their best work to catalyze strategic, equity-oriented improvement.

Acknowledgments

We would like to thank our colleagues who have spurred our thinking about the practice of coaching, why coaching is important, and its ties to strategy, continuous improvement, professional learning, policy, and equity. These include Sarah Birkeland, Mario Carullo, Cynthia Coburn, David Eddy-Spicer, Rachael Gabriel, John Hall, Rydell Harrison, Ayesha Hashim, Coach Heiser, Britney Jones, Richard Lemons, Alli Leslie, Ann O'Doherty, Jessica Rigby, Michele Tissiere, Tina Trujillo, Andrew Volkert, Jennie Weiner, and Max Yurkofsky.

Pursuing joy while aiming to expand the field's understanding of coaching, we are grateful for excellent coffee, breakfast tacos, kitchen windows filled with foliage and light, deep belly breaths, running shoes, great books, wonderful podcasts, and really good bread.

CHAPTER 1

Introducing How and Why Coaching Matters

Whatever ails a district or school—insufficient progress as measured by standardized tests, inconsistent science instruction, inequitable discipline approaches, ineffective leadership—coaching is prescribed as a solution. Coaching has become the wonder drug of education. Coaches are supposed to be experts in curriculum, instruction, data analysis, and leadership, and they are expected to understand and navigate the intricacies of reforms, organizational learning, and adult learning. Coaches are tasked with an assortment of duties while holding limited formal power, and often encounter barriers for enacting plans. Without clarity about what they are coaching toward, and in the absence of a system-wide strategy for educational improvement, coaches' hands are tied. Lack of clarity, communication, and strategy regarding coaching does not affect only coaches. Indeed, teachers and leaders also feel unsure how—and why—to participate in coaching. These conditions place coaches and their clients in a muddle of distrust and inefficiencies that is unlikely to produce meaningful improvement.

Coaching is often overpromised and underutilized. That is, coaching is heralded as solving many issues—from teachers' implementation of a mathematics curriculum to student engagement and principal retention—but the systems and culture for coaching are lacking. The resources, guidelines, and schedules of districts and schools fail to enable coaches to engage in key aspects of their work. And the culture regarding adult learning and organizational improvement may not embrace or align to coaching. Coaching *should* tightly align with strategic improvement and professional learning efforts; however, coaching is often only loosely tied to those efforts. In *Making Coaching Matter,* we grapple with how to connect coaching with strategic, equitable improvement. The purpose of this book is to illuminate how to strengthen the infrastructure for coaching so the education system can make better use of coaching to foster and sustain positive change.

This is not a book about coaching, in the sense that it is not a book for coaches, or other educators, who want to learn how to coach. Nor do we elaborate on discrete components of coaching, such as listening, questioning, or feedback. Additionally, this book is not a manifesto for a single coaching model. Indeed, although we have strong opinions about what constitutes good coaching, we don't advance one model over another; our definition of coaching makes for a big tent. We articulate, therefore, the coaching model employed should be designed for the purpose it is intended to serve. Moreover, we think all models benefit from strong, coherent infrastructure for coaching.

Instead, this book provides ideas to assist in making coaching a powerful support for educational organizations' strategy for improvement, as well as a vehicle for individual professional learning. We encourage you to reflect on the assumptions embedded in the structures and practices of coaching in your context. To that end, we share concepts, structures, and activities for strengthening coaching programs and bringing clarity to coaching to enable coaches to engage in high-leverage practices and foster strategic, equitable learning and improvement.

CHALLENGES FOR COACHING

Over the last few years, we have had several experiences with districts in which coaches have been hired to fix a problem such as low math test scores. The theory of action in these cases is commonly assumed as, "if we hire teachers who are effective and ask them to coach other teachers, then teaching practices will improve, and there will be improvements in student learning." Within this, we hear many assumptions, including that the effective teachers have skills that can be transferred to others, as well as that being an effective teacher means being an effective coach. We also detect assumptions that teachers find time for coaching and will respond well to coaching, and that coaches will receive necessary training and support. Our experience, however, is that these assumptions on coaching are rarely explored or accounted for.

Further, we have had several conversations with a disappointed or frustrated superintendent who realizes that they have invested millions of dollars in coaching, with few successes to speak of. Unfortunately, superintendents are likely to blame coaches rather than accept that these issues are *not* the coaches' fault; rather, the systems, or infrastructure, necessary for strategic, equitable, and successful coaching had not been designed or implemented to enable coaching to drive improvement.

The lackluster results mentioned above signal that coaching is rarely optimized to achieve its objectives: individual learning and organizational improvement. As practitioners and researchers, we have seen loose ties between strategic plans and coaching and weak guidance for coaches on how to carry out their work. The working conditions for coaches may not be optimal. Stemming from this, coaching and coaches' work aims toward different targets. Further, coaching differs across schools—and sometimes even inside one school. Because there are multiple, murky definitions of coaching, it is tricky to scale up, support, and evaluate coaching. As such, coaching frequently does not yield its desired outcomes.

Merely launching a coaching program and hiring coaches does little to enable improvement. Similarly, putting the "coach" label on a person or position in a school does not transform their work into coaching, does not improve outcomes, and does not make their work kinder, friendlier, or more effective. Thus, we ask ourselves: How can we strengthen coaching and support coaches to enable strategic, equitable improvement? How can we optimize coaching so coaches can catalyze equitable improvement? How can we ensure coaching matters?

Across our work, we have noticed that many district leaders and principals lack clarity on how to best deploy coaches, resulting in coaching programs existing on paper yet failing to be enacted purposefully in practice. In some cases, coaching programs are loosely defined, and coaches receive little guidance (Woulfin, 2020). In other cases, there are mismatches between the coaching initiative, coaches' work, and strategic priorities (Coburn & Woulfin, 2012; Galey-Horn & Woulfin, 2021). The gaps in implementing coaching result in district and school leaders misdiagnosing problems, making false assumptions about the influence of coaches' work and the impact of a coaching model, and failing to see problems at the organizational and/or system levels. These misfirings matter, especially as coaching is a resource-intensive improvement lever. For instance, mid-sized public school districts may spend $2–3 million per year on coaching salaries, and they expect significant changes in outcomes from this significant investment. This book confronts these realities and barriers to fully realizing the promise of coaching; it offers insights on infrastructure to create and sustain strategic, equity-centered coaching.

NESTED NOTIONS OF COACHING

Coaching is both a tool for improving individual practice and for improving an organization. When considering coaching at the individual level, it is a method of supporting, in the short term, a person's decision-making and action in pursuit of a defined goal. And, in the longer term, coaching can develop the person's capacity to self-regulate; that is, to generate and stay focused on a goal, to self-assess where they are in relation to that goal, and to figure out what they should do as next steps to reach the goal. The essential function of the coach is to scaffold the client's thinking by asking questions and providing feedback. But coaching—similar to ballet,

Figure 1.1. Nested definitions of coaching at the individual, organizational, and system levels.

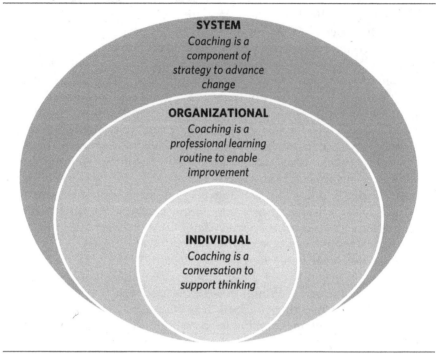

SYSTEM
Coaching is a component of strategy to advance change

ORGANIZATIONAL
Coaching is a professional learning routine to enable improvement

INDIVIDUAL
Coaching is a conversation to support thinking

mountain climbing, and, of course, teaching—is a craft shaped by the context and conditions.

Coaching holds the potential to encourage improvement at the individual, organizational, and system levels. We argue it holds the greatest promise when attention is paid to all three. Figure 1.1 represents the way coaching possesses different definitions when examined from individual-, organizational-, and system-level stances. These definitions are important because, as discussed, educators oftentimes think of coaching only at the individual level, with fewer considerations of the compounding factors across all levels.

The techniques that coaches use to support client thinking, at the individual level, align to tenets of psychology, including but not limited to self-regulation, goal-setting behavior, and perceived self-efficacy (Aguilar, 2013; Costa & Garmston, 2015). Moving to the organizational level, coaching is a system for professional learning that involves ongoing, contextualized professional development aligned to the goals of the organization, such as implementing a new math program or improving leadership techniques (Bean, 2015; Joyce & Showers, 1981). Additionally, coaching can function as an instrument for advancing organizational change. At the system level, coaching is a branch of strategy that enables the organization to reach major goals by building capacity, focusing the work, and obtaining evidence to refine the strategy and improve its levers.

To optimize coaching, reformers and administrators should not simply attend to coaching at a single level (i.e., system, organizational, or individual) but, rather, attend to the nature of, conditions for, and alignment of coaching across all levels. For example, to ensure one-on-one leadership coaching is well received, advancing a principal's social justice leadership practices, it is necessary to check the organizational conditions for leadership coaching and the system-level policies and funding shaping leadership coaching. Or, to ensure coaching on a statewide reading reform is optimized, it is necessary to consider the school-level conditions for professional learning on reading as well as the nature of reading coaches' work.

REFORMING SCHOOLS UNDER PRESSURE

We attend to the accountability policy context and inequities of the education system because these are powerful forces continually shaping the design and implementation of coaching programs plus coaches' work. Districts and schools face continual pressure to change via layers of reform and pressures to improve; Chapter 3 offers additional details on policy movements over time. Recently, states and districts have adopted new, challenging academic standards and innovative instructional approaches to prepare children and youth for participating in work and society (Horsford et al., 2018; Peurach et al., 2019). Implementing these standards and approaches necessitates changing numerous facets and activities of central office, the principalship, coaching, teacher professional development, and instruction. Simultaneously, district and school leaders face accountability pressure to demonstrate, or "prove," the effectiveness of their schools and teachers (Trujillo, 2013; Woulfin et al., 2016). Making change under pressure is not the smoothest process!

Making change is also rocky because our educational system is inequitable and woefully under-resourced (Baker, 2021; Horsford et al., 2018). Racist and ableist structures—and pernicious, deep-seated, beliefs about who deserves and benefits from different types of instructional and educational experiences—influence all aspects of schools, including coaching (Annamma et al., 2017; Ladson-Billings, 2021). Longstanding racialized disparities in funding for schooling and the hollowing out of social services (e.g., healthcare) across the United States result in harmful inequalities within and across school communities (Baker, 2021; Jackson, 2020; Thorson & Gearhart, 2019). Schools, teachers, and leaders are doing more, oftentimes with less. This places stress on educational organizations, leaders, and teachers, contributing to challenges in recruiting and retaining educators (Billingsley & Bettini, 2019; Bristol, 2020). Leaders and teachers desire, and benefit from, greater support, particularly to advance substantive change.

To meet new expectations and close gaps in learning opportunities, state and district administrators have adopted new instructional programs, devoted attention to new approaches, and launched new professional development. For example, district administrators select and promote new instructional materials, assessments, and intervention programs addressing mathematics as well as meeting the needs of English learners (Elfers & Stritikus, 2014; Handsman et al., 2022). Other administrators seek to reveal opportunity gaps and attempt to shift mindsets on race and racism; this may involve professional development sessions, educator book clubs, and webinars (Bocala & Boudett, 2022; Diem & Welton, 2020; Welton et al., 2018). And districts and schools adopted laptops, iPads, and numerous online programs before and during the COVID-19 era as digital tools to shift the nature of teaching and create new ways of doing school (Bartlett, 2022; Lamb & Weiner, 2021; Stelitano et al., 2020).

These reforms introduce ideas, guidelines, tools, and routines for leaders, teachers, and staff. Each reform could be advanced by ongoing, contextualized learning opportunities and time and space for enactment, monitoring, and refinement, so it fits with local conditions and needs. For these reasons, coaching can play a key role in translating these reforms. More concretely, aligning coaches' work with each of these reforms aids leaders and teachers to deeply enact a wide set of initiatives in strategic, equitable ways.

We underscore the complexity of implementing multiple reforms. Educators face clashing messages on reforms, and the "too-muchness" of adopting several initiatives contributes to burnout. Consequently, there are teacher recruitment and retention problems as well as problematic diversity issues for the teacher and leader pipelines (Noonan & Bristol, 2020). For these reasons, there is a pressing need for district and school leaders to leverage coaching to help resolve these complex issues in thoughtful, supportive ways. In the following section, we direct attention to the nature and popularity of coaching as a lever for reform. Within this, we begin operationalizing how coaching is an engine for organizational change.

THE RISE OF COACHING

Coaching has proliferated, been lauded as the reform *du jour,* and studied from several angles. It is nearly impossible *not* to notice the spread and reach of coaching: from executive, nutrition, and parenting coaches to reading and math coaches, district science coaches, and equity coaches (Chapter 8 delves into the spectrum of coaching). In the education field, district leaders and coaches often articulate the value of coaching for enabling professional learning. Reformers boast how coaching supports teachers and accelerates improvement. Reformers and administrators also articulate that coaching functions as the next rung on educators' career ladder, potentially aiding in retaining effective educators. However, coaching has some drawbacks, including its cost as a reform lever, because it adds a new position to the district/school (Knight, 2012).

Coaching is one form of professional learning. That is, pre-service training, professional development for teachers and leaders, new teacher induction, professional learning communities, and coaching *all* provide professional learning opportunities (Coburn, 2001; Garet et al., 2001; Penuel et al., 2007). In this way, coaches are one source of professional learning for educators. Importantly, coaches can (and should!) extend and reinforce ideas from educators' other professional development opportunities (Coburn & Russell, 2008; Matsumura et al., 2013; Woulfin, 2018).

At the system level, coaching is a reform itself—with its own rules, norms, resources, and roles (Woulfin, 2020). That is, a coaching model operates as a vehicle for professional development as well as a leadership structure that promotes change. Moving to the organizational level, coaching involves organizational change, with the coach facilitating teams of educators and collaborating with leaders to advance change (Aguilar, 2016).

For example, coaching can foster schoolwide adoption of a reading instructional model, leading to consistent approaches to instruction across the building. And principal coaching can help advance disctrictwide organizational change in how the district approaches family involvement. Lastly, at the individual level, coaching entails a coach supporting, instructing, and advising other educators with a great deal of reflection (Aguilar, 2013).

Coaching provides contextualized, specialized, and ongoing professional learning opportunities, and it matches tenets of effective professional development (Garet et al., 2001; Penuel et al., 2007). Coaches can be embedded in educational organizations, with contextual knowledge and skills to foster reflection and learning over time. Taken together, coaching must be optimized so coaches can play a role in expanding educators' knowledge and skills related to strategic priorities.

Researchers have answered multiple questions on the relationship between coaching and education policy and practice. First, researchers determined there was a major rise in employing instructional specialists in the early 2000s (Domina et al., 2015). Many districts instituted coaching as a lever to drive change and work toward accountability goals; Chapter 3 explores the rise of coaching. Second, researchers identified positive impacts of coaching, such as coaching affecting changes in teachers' classroom practice and patterns in student achievement (Coburn & Woulfin, 2012; Kraft et al. 2018; Matsumura et al., 2013). There is strong evidence that coaches assist teachers in developing understandings of and carrying out instructional strategies.

Third, researchers illuminated how district and school conditions and leadership affect the nature of coaching and coaches' work: first, how district leaders define coaching influences what coaching looks like for educators and its effects on practice (Mangin, 2009; Mangin & Dusmore, 2015; Woulfin, 2020); second, a school's norms regarding leadership, teachers' work, and instructional improvement influence coaches' work. There is mounting evidence that a district's ecosystem, infrastructure, and strategic plan shapes coaching models, coaches' work, and ultimately, educators' responses to coaching (Coburn & Russell, 2008; Stevenson & Weiner, 2020). Across chapters, we draw on recent scholarship on coaching to bolster points on how to optimize coaching programs and improve coaches' work to attain deep objectives.

THE WORK OF COACHES

Administrators turn to coaching to improve multiple outcomes, with coaches engaging in multiple activities to develop educators' work toward change. Traditionally, coaches and their coaching targeted instructional improvement. For example, mathematics coaches focus on strengthening the adoption of math curricula, math instruction, and math achievement (Coburn & Russell, 2008; Gibbons & Cobb, 2017). And English learner (EL) coaches focus on providing support to teachers around how to plan and instruct EL students in a manner aligned with current research on responsive, engaging approaches to support ELs. Notably, coaching programs also focus on other components of schooling; for instance, as described in Chapter 8, there are behavior coaches and leadership coaches. In particular, principal coaching emerged to assist in bolstering instructional leadership and equity-focused leadership with an eye toward supporting principals and meeting accountability goals (Aguilar et al., 2011; Bickman et al., 2012; Lochmiller, 2014). Regardless of whether coaching teachers on facets of instruction or coaching principals on leadership elements, it is vital to bolster coaching at the individual, organizational, and system levels to maximize its influence and impact.

Coaches wear many hats, and teacher coaching, as a lever for improvement, is framed by practitioners and researchers in multiple ways. Some portray coaching as *breaking down the classroom door to increase transparency about instruction*, foster consistent instruction across classrooms, and improve student outcomes. This framing highlights coaches' role in observing instruction, developing capacity around teaching, and promoting specific changes in teaching. And some portray coaching as *leading change to catalyze reform*, with coaches positioned as quasi-administrators facilitating collaboration, curriculum design and implementation, and data analysis. In this framing, coaches lead teams of teachers to analyze data, set plans to meet goals, and engage in lesson planning and/or professional learning activities. Others portray coaching as *enabling educators to blossom*. In this framing, coaches mentor others, providing individualized support, which may not relate to initiatives yet encourages individualized growth and educator retention. Others even portray coaching as *leading teachers informally*. The teacher leadership framing embraces the notion that teachers can support each other's improvement and increase buy-in for schoolwide change. We underscore that infrastructure and leadership are necessary for optimizing each of these framings of coaching.

STRATEGIC COACHING

We care about coaching not only because coaches do important, intriguing work, but because coaching moves schools to function as learning organizations and can be melded with strategic, equity-centered goals. Emphasizing that centering equity in educational improvement involves both individual and collective conversations, in this book we highlight that coaches have a unique capacity to engage in these efforts. And we care deeply about ensuring coaches engage in equity-centered work.

In addition to building the capacity of individuals and teams of educators, coaching plays a role in strategic improvement. By strategic, we mean the alignment of goals, resources, people, and practices (Stevenson & Weiner, 2021). We emphasize that strategy requires leaders, including district leaders, principals, and coaches, to work in concert toward goals. For instance, if Purple District's strategic goal is to raise middle school students' writing skills and achievement, instructional coaches would provide aligned PD on writing, facilitate teachers' lesson planning on writing, observe teachers' writing instruction, provide individualized support as teachers encounter obstacles in writing instruction, and communicate with district and school leaders about strengths and areas of opportunity with regard to teachers' writing instruction. This means coaches would discuss the writing reform with principals. Notably, there is a throughline for this coaching—reaching the goal of improving teachers' writing instruction and the level of students' writing proficiency. There is also consistency in what coaches are doing within and across schools to build individual and organizational capacity related to writing instruction. In this context, district leaders, principals, teachers, and coaches would all hold clear understandings of how and why coaches are focused on writing instructional improvement.

Strategic coaching involves asking: What are the broad goals of the district/school? It is then necessary to specify what coaches will strive to improve to help reach particular targets: Teachers' pedagogical routines? Teacher retention? Leaders' approaches to parent engagement? Students' ELA test scores? Students' SEL competencies? In this manner, strategy and coaching are braided together. In this book, we explain how coaching moderates strategy, encouraging simultaneous attention to system goals and the activities of coaching to advance crucial change. We underscore that editing coaches' job descriptions or providing a single workshop to principals on coaching is insufficient for maximizing coaching. It is necessary to assemble infrastructure for coaching and engage in ongoing leadership that frames and elevates coaching.

In sum, coaching is a lever for purposefully advancing the organization's strategic goals. By amplifying major goals and supporting adult learning on how and why to take steps toward those goals, coaching can further coherence—so everyone moves in concert toward those goals (Woulfin & Rigby, 2017). While engaging in those activities, coaches can detect—and diagnose—other issues. Thus, coaches are pivotal for district and school-based continuous improvement efforts. Further, if a coaching program is floundering, this is a signal—for district and school leaders—of other organizational and system issues. If coaching has not yielded desired outcomes, it is quite likely due to gaps in strategic planning, leadership, and professional learning rather than due to the capacity and motivation of individual coaches. For these reasons, we urge bolstering the infrastructure for strategic, equity-centered coaching.

CONCLUSION

This chapter provided background information on how and why coaching matters for the field of education. Within this chapter, we discussed the differing and, at times competing, models for and conceptions of coaching—with consequences for how teachers and other educators make sense of this reform instrument. We remind leaders, therefore, of their role in clearly defining coaching and, more broadly, designing infrastructure that enables strategic, equity-centered coaching. While highlighting the potential for coaching to promote learning and change, the chapter acknowledges systemic barriers constraining coaches' work and, in turn, preventing coaching from reaching its target. In the following chapter, we dig into facets of coaches' work, devoting attention to how coaches actively create trustful relationships through enacting coaching routines. Chapter 2 also discusses the theory-based roots of coaching so that leaders can refine the nature of coaching routines, including questioning, listening, and providing feedback.

The Craft of Coaching

It's the little details that are vital. Little things make big things happen.

—John Wooden

Our author team recognizes that there are many factors enabling strategic, equity-centered coaching, including a coach's practices or "moves," the systems and supports for coaching in an organization, and the norms regarding coaching. This chapter focuses on the first of these factors: components of coaches' work, or the craft of strategic, equity-centered coaching. However, we trumpet that, although a coach's activities matter, it is crucial to treat coaching as part of a larger strategy, rather than an activity unto itself.

Coaching revolves around service to others—as choosing to put cognitive and emotional time and effort into supporting others' work—so that they are better positioned to lead, teach, and develop capacity in their colleagues, with the ultimate aim of equitable student outcomes. Therefore, it is a moral endeavor; it works toward a lofty and worthy aim—to increase the sum total of good in the world. If we deem education as a lever for reducing inequity, then coaches must do their part through equity-centered coaching.

At times, educators hear the phrase "coaching for equity," and may think that only applies to educators in schools with a high percentage of students of color or students from poverty. We worry this phrase leads to educators thinking of coaching for equity as distinct from instructional or leadership coaching. But we do not know of any districts where there are not disparities of some kind in the opportunities students are offered, the experiences they are exposed to, and the achievements they accrue. Further, if we, as coaches, are not always coaching for equity, that means we are sometimes coaching for inequity. As such, concepts related to equity are always fundamental, and all educators should continually improve practices to work toward equity in their classrooms, schools, and communities.

So, what should coaches do to promote learning, catalyze change, and make coaching matter? There are many coaching models that apply many different approaches to coaching, from real-time, task-oriented models that rely on an expert giving feedback, to content-neutral models that envision the coach as providing support only for the thinking, and not the knowledge or skills, of the client. Therefore, we purposefully offer an all-encompassing discussion of coaching. We do so because, despite the dozens, perhaps hundreds, of coaching models enshrined in books, websites, and mini-conferences, they all depend on some fundamental theoretical constructs and coaching skills that we describe in this chapter.

In the early days of psychotherapy, Rosenzweig (1936) pointed out that despite the existence of many different schools of therapy, they all had more in common than they had distinctions from one other. We view coaching in much the same way; there are many models that ultimately share many features. It is possible to overstate how different the different coaching models are from one another, partly because it behooves the purveyor of a particular model to emphasize how distinct and better their model is from all the lesser ones out there. For us, coaching is a big tent, so the differences among models are much less important than the pragmatic effort to meet the needs of real-life practitioners whose work we, as coaches, are trying to support.

Moreover, coaching is a craft (Aguilar, 2013). Coaching, like teaching, looks deceptively easy, yet it is extraordinarily difficult to do well. It requires a great deal of knowledge: of how people think; of the barriers they may come across and the traps they may fall into; of the constructs that are useful in helping them analyze the world and design plans; of the possibilities for improvement. It also requires a great deal of skill because every coaching conversation is a little different: The problem is different, the people are different, the context is different. The coach, therefore, is bringing to bear all of their knowledge and skill in a highly responsive way. The coach is also holding in mind the overarching purpose, which is the vision and mission of the organization. In education, the ultimate purpose is always about ensuring the success of all students. And the success of all students leads to a discussion of coaching for equity. We also want to draw your attention to what is NOT in this chapter. There are no:

- visuals of coaching models;
- narratives of coaching cycles; and
- forms to fill out.

Instead, this chapter delves into multiple dimensions of the craft of coaching, including the role of relationships, mental models associated with coaching, and, finally, bedrock coaching practices.

RELATIONSHIPS IN AND FOR COACHING

They don't care how much you know, unless they know how much you care.

—Pat Summitt

When we work with educators who are interested in becoming coaches, and with leaders who are interested in developing a coaching model, one of the maxims that we hear repeatedly is that "coaching is all about relationships." We nod, since it is certainly the case that coaching is not possible without a respectful and trusting relationship between coach and client. However, we see and hear across frequent misunderstandings about what such a relationship entails, how to create positive relationships, and what results from such relationships. In this chapter, we explain how and why jumping into the core routines of coaching with a clear, strategic purpose, in lieu of tiptoeing through introductions or relationship-building, bolsters the implementation of coaching.

An idea that we hear a lot is that coaches should "build a relationship" or "build trust" *before* they can coach someone. We call this the Relationship Fallacy. Let's think it through. For example, say that a coach watches a teacher and realizes that she is calling on boys much more often than girls, but does not say anything because he feels like they do not yet have a relationship, or that he does not want to damage trust. So, when is an opportune time for the coach to say something? And when the coach does say something, how long is it going to take the teacher to figure out that he has been keeping information from her for a while? That seems to us to be a recipe for a *lack* of trust.

Or, let's imagine that a leadership coach hears a principal's plans for the next staff professional development (PD) session and has concerns about how it will be received by the staff, but she does not say anything because she feels like they do not yet have a relationship, or that she does not want to damage trust. And let's say that, indeed, the PD doesn't go well, and the principal realizes that her coach could have said something but chose not to. It is hard to imagine that the principal would not feel let down—perhaps even angry or betrayed—when she finds out that her coach chose to not give the feedback on the PD. Feeling disappointed by one's coach is not a great recipe for a productive relationship. Not saying what you think, therefore, is risky due to a faulty assumption: that people can be offended when you tell them how you see things, and that you need to "have a relationship with them" before it is appropriate to provide feedback.

We see it differently. It's not sharing evidence or providing feedback that causes offense. Instead, it is acting in a way that is not in the best interest of the other person. It is possible to cause offense by what you say, but whether or not you cause offense is less dependent on how well you know the person than whether the other person believes that your intentions are benevolent. The coach, therefore, must be willing and able to enter into a coaching relationship *in service of* the other person. In addition, length of time is not the determining factor when it comes to demonstrating benevolence; our contention is that a skillful coach is able to signal very early on in a coaching engagement that they hold the interests of the coachee paramount.

In our experience, the way to build trust is to demonstrate clearly and unambiguously *from the very beginning* that you are a competent professional and decent human being who holds the best interests of your client front and center in your thinking and speaking (Munson & Saclarides, 2022). The only way you can demonstrate that is to tell the truth as you see it, which may include providing information that you think your client may find hard to hear. The only way to demonstrate competence is to be a competent coach, and that includes the ability to have a potentially awkward conversation! The only way to demonstrate benevolence is to act in the best interest of your client, which includes understanding what they value and telling them what you think they ought to know. In other words, the only way to build a relationship is to be trustworthy, and the only way to be trustworthy is to be honest and transparent in a manner that builds trust rather than undermining it.

More concretely, a coach cultivates a trusting relationship by applying the following traits:

- Being reliable and trustworthy
- Maintaining confidentiality
- Being open and transparent
- Working to see a situation through the client's eyes
- Acting in the client's best interest
- Helping the client recognize additional areas for professional growth

A relationship, however, is not one-sided, and the coachee helps foster the relationship by doing the following:

- Being open about struggles
- Letting the coach see the client at work—a coach is not much use during a performance, but is invaluable during rehearsal, and especially during the post-performance critique when the performance was not particularly smooth
- Following through with scheduled appointments and between-visit commitments

- Adopting a "learner stance"—working to be okay with confusion, mixed messages, and ambiguity as the coach will not necessarily provide the "right answer"
- Taking ownership—seeking to bring problems within the client's circle of control. This is a skill that the coach can help the client think through

TRUST

Coupled with the notion of relationships, there are many definitions of trust (e.g., Bryk & Schneider, 2002; Tschannen-Moran, 2004). We define trust as being built from three components: personal characteristics (are you reliable, honest, and good?); competence (do you do your job well consistently and predictably?); and benevolence (will you support me if things go sideways?). You can separate these from each other (I can be a nice person but incompetent), but you cannot meaningfully separate them from the operational setting—trusting me as a good middle school principal does not mean that you will trust me as a good surgeon. Trust, therefore, is built by engaging the work together, not by learning where someone grew up and if they enjoy watching sports or have children.

Notably, these categories overlap—reliability, for example, is both a personal characteristic and an aspect of job performance. And compassion is often a personal characteristic, an essential part of being an educator, and a key component in a relationship. Trust is also situation-specific. I may trust you to take care of my dog, but not to keep something confidential. With regard to trust, context matters.

Trust intersects with components of coaching, particularly feedback. Telling someone "the truth" sometimes feels like it jeopardizes a personal relationship, because the feedback receiver may feel that the feedback shows a lack of benevolence on the part of the feedback giver. The coach, therefore, needs to cultivate ways of giving feedback that build trust rather than threatening it. For example, the line, "I'm giving you these comments because I have very high expectations and I know that you can reach them" was used as part of a study of "wise" feedback with high school students; the students whose feedback from teachers was preceded with this phrase were far more likely to revise their work (Yeager et al., 2014). Thus, as a coach, waiting to build a relationship before giving feedback undermines trust, as the client often realizes that you are withholding information.

Evaluation can nudge people toward protecting themselves from being found as having gaps or weaknesses, which encourages them to be seen at their best. Coaching, however, involves people being willing to be seen at their worst, and so a trusting relationship in which educators are willing to talk about their unvarnished work should be free of evaluation. Just like the students in Yeager et al.'s study, educators should believe that their coach has faith in them, and that the coaching conversation is the vehicle through which they move closer to the high performance level their coach believes them to be capable of.

The language we use when talking about trust shapes the way we think about it. We encourage thinking of trust as pliable, or elastic, and capable of regaining its shape after being stretched. This is a further reminder that we have to be willing to be optimistic in our interactions with others. Both coaches and clients, therefore, should hold faith that their investments of time and energy into coaching will yield dividends, believe that people are doing the best they know how to do, not read too much into any given interaction, and not infer that one misstep denotes malevolence. Trust mediates coaching in several ways, and it is also important to shed light on mental models that color and guide coaches' work.

MENTAL MODELS FOR COACHING

While treating coaching as a craft, we note that coaching is not atheoretical. Coaching aligns with multiple theories; it is a bricolage of constructs united by a philosophy of faith in people to learn, change, and improve. Moreover, coaches deploy their internal theories to act for reasons that they believe to be true as a result of their actions. Some of these theories have been constructed out of personal experience, and some adopted or adapted from psychology and sociology.

There is a large body of research in social psychology and behavioral economics showing that humans rely on incomplete representations of the world to operate efficiently in it; we simply cannot cope with the enormous volume of data that we are exposed to at all times, and we need ways of sorting and simplifying the data so that we can cope with it (Kahneman, 2011; Ross & Nisbett, 2011). This makes us rapid and competent problem-solvers, but it also means that we try to fit discomfiting facts into existing stories that we tell ourselves about how the world works—these incomplete versions of reality are known as mental models.

Mental models are essential in allowing us to move smoothly through the world, but they also contribute to making assumptions about people and situations that may not be warranted. We move quickly from the inputs we are aware of—not realizing that we have filtered the data in such a way that reinforces already held beliefs—to making assumptions, to drawing conclusions, to acting on what we believe to be true, even though that version of the truth may be only one of many possibilities. In this section, we provide insights on ladder of inference and self-efficacy as mental models interlinked with coaching. Ladder of inference describes how people process and ultimately draw conclusions from information. Secondly, self-efficacy concentrates on the way that feeling effective is an ingredient motivating improvement efforts. We depict how these two mental models are braided with coaches' work in important ways.

Ladder of Inference

The ladder of inference, developed by Chris Argyris (1990), explains how people select and interpret the facts available to them. It is a useful tool to analyze the assumptions we tend to make about the world. The ladder of inference is both a distillation of several psychological constructs (including confirmation bias, or the tendency to favor information that confirms our existing mental models, and the stereotypes we hold about people based on characteristics such as age, race, and physical ability) and a communication tool. In particular, the ladder of inference gives coaches a way of talking with their client about the mental processes that allow them to see the world not as it really is (which is actually impossible) but as they think it already is. In turn, this affords entry points into conversation about various forms of evidence and how they could shape future action.

Using the ladder of inference, coaching questions could include, "I hear you making several assumptions about what's really going on here. Can we maybe identify those and see if there aren't alternative explanations?", or "I know that solution is the one that seems most likely to work, but can we just take a couple of minutes to generate what other options you have?" Notably, by pausing to ask these questions, the coach provides an opportunity for a coachee to reflect on alternate interpretations of current conditions or evidence and expand the nature of responses to solve issues. As such, when coaches draw on ladder of inference, they account for how people construct judgments of information or evidence. Next, we point to the ways coaches can acknowledge and address how the willingness of individuals to make change is influenced by perceptions of their own effectiveness.

Self-Efficacy

Perceived self-efficacy is a theory, described by psychologist Albert Bandura (1977), explaining our decision to act in any given situation. Bandura (1977) wrote: "Efficacy expectations determine how much effort people will expend and how long they will persist in the face of obstacles and aversive experiences. The stronger the perceived self-efficacy, the more active the efforts." (p. 194). These issues of efficacy are woven with coaching and coaches' work to motivate coachees to try new behaviors to reach

Figure 2.1. Bandura's model of how self-efficacy mediates the activities and outcomes of a person.

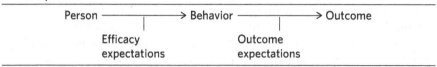

specific outcomes. Figure 2.1 shows that whether individuals attempt to achieve a goal depends on the following two beliefs:

1. Whether they believe that they are capable of adequately performing the behavior needed to reach the outcome (efficacy expectations)
2. Whether they believe that if they perform the behavior adequately, it will get them the outcome they are hoping for (outcome expectations)

Across contexts, people faced with a challenging goal assess the likelihood that they can reach that goal by exercising the skills that they have. Bandura's theory explains people's motivation to achieve some goals and not others, and why some people persist and some give up. Individuals with high self-efficacy are more likely to choose loftier goals, to see a failure as a temporary setback, and to persist in trying to meet their goal. Self-efficacy is about agency: It describes the circumstances under which we believe we can make a difference.

Bandura's model suggests that people are motivated to work toward a particular goal when they believe the goal is achievable and that they are capable of enacting the skills needed to achieve the goal. This strongly suggests, therefore, that an approach limited to teachers' personal awareness of equity and inequity (i.e., the "person" part of Bandura's model) or increasing expectations for students (i.e., "outcome expectations"), is not adequate for building the knowledge and skills teachers need to improve their "efficacy expectations."

In coaching, using the self-efficacy framework gives a construct, and language, to talk about assumptions, expectations, and areas for growth. It is not unusual for a new principal, for example, to tell their leadership coach that they did not do something that they know they "ought" to do because "it's not going to work." Maybe they didn't talk to the teacher who didn't show up for lunch duty, or to the custodian who yelled at a 4th-grader. The reasons are frequently framed as outcome expectations: "I know her and she's not going to change," or "he's retiring at the end of the year anyway."

When a coach hears a coachee express lack of faith that a result can be achieved, self-efficacy is useful for analyzing what could underlie that lack of faith and then thinking about other steps that might increase the odds of shifting practice. A coaching question, when using the self-efficacy model, might be:

> So I hear you express unwillingness to have a heart-to-heart with that teacher. Is that because you really believe that he is a hopeless case, or is it possible that you just are not sure how to go about having that conversation with him?

The coach might offer to role-play such a conversation, so that the principal goes into the conversation better prepared, is more likely to obtain a satisfactory result, and is therefore more likely to attempt such a conversation in the future. In illustrations of how coaches might deploy the mental models of self-efficacy, as well as ladder of inference, we presented examples of coaches listening, questioning, and sharing feedback to support improvement. Next, we delve into features of these bedrock coaching practices—with particular attention to how coaches promote strategic, equity-oriented changes through these moves.

BEDROCK COACHING PRACTICES

In this section, we discuss fundamental, high-leverage coaching practices: listening, questioning, setting goals, and providing feedback. We portray how coaches engage in these practices while also explaining how each practice operates in the service on strategic, equity-centered coaching.

Listening

Being a good listener is frequently cited as key to becoming a better leader, parent, and colleague. Listening is certainly a skill not limited to coaching; although in our experience, coaching is where there is purposeful development of the skill. And listening, even though it feels like a passive—or even easy—skill to conduct turns out to be very demanding. Within coaching, listening is important for several reasons. First, everyone wants to feel that they are listened to. Listening is a mark of respect, an acknowledgment that what a person has to say is important, and an invitation to think together. Therefore, if coaching is to exist as a productive relationship, listening is crucial.

Second, when a coachee states their ideas aloud, it helps make their thinking more concrete. Additionally, a coach can garner evidence on current practices and beliefs. We highlight it is the role of the coach to scaffold these spoken ideas: to track what is said, so that it can be held up, examined, pulled apart, and put back together again. This can only happen if the coach is listening closely to the thoughts expressed. Third, listening well communicates several things: that thinking is valued, that listening is important, that it is worth devoting time to reaching a shared understanding, and that planning and strategizing require discipline and routines. Listening is difficult because it is both cognitively demanding and requires self-management on the part of the listener. The cognitive demand is a result of paying close attention and making sense of what is being said. The self-management is necessary to overcome the natural tendency of the listener to relate what is being said to their own experience, and to either respond based on those connections, or to stop paying attention to the speaker because they are taken up with their own thoughts.

In coaching, listening is *the* absolute bedrock practice. If the objective of the coach is to support the progress of educators toward their goals by supporting their thinking, then being able to listen closely to discern their mental models, aspirations, values, assumptions, biases, concerns, and rationales is crucial. In optimized coaching models, coaches are selected, developed, and supported to listen to coachees with the underlying goal of promoting individual and organizational learning.

Questioning

In addition to listening, questioning is another practice central to coaching. We have noticed that a preoccupation of novice coaches is asking "good questions." In particular, when we ask workshop participants to set an intention for what coaches would like to learn more about, they will frequently say, "I want to ask better questions." And when we debrief coaching demonstrations, coaches will often ask, "How did you know that was the right question to ask?" Our response is always, "There is no good or bad question; there is only what happens in the mind of the client." In other words, the idea that a question is good or bad separate from the client's response is missing the point.

The purpose of questioning is to help the coachee think through what action they want to take in order to reach a goal. There are, therefore, many possible, necessary, intermediate questions that challenge assumptions, clarify thinking about goals and theory of action, and so on. So, questioning can be two things at once: It can be the prompt to solicit useful information about another's thinking, and it can also be an intervention in itself. After a coach asks a question and listens thoughtfully to the response, they can learn how the coachee is making sense of strengths and challenges and what types of changes they are considering attempting. In turn, the coach can clarify issues as well as provide aligned supports.

One of the reasons that asking good questions is hard is that the questioner (frequently a formal superior, such as a director or principal) tends to think that the purpose of questioning is to lead the other person (frequently a formal supervisee, such as a teacher) to a predetermined outcome. They ask leading questions because they think they already have the answer and that by asking leading questions, they will help the client see things their way, and will have more "buy-in" if they "get there by themselves." This, of course, assumes that the "there" they have in mind is the correct answer, and so learning to ask good questions also involves letting go of some preconceived ideas about who the expert is and who holds authority in any given conversation. More concretely, asking good questions involves shifting away from quizzing or interviewing the coachee.

We encourage educators to think of questioning in terms greater than the individual question they ask. Rather, educators should think of questions not as individual miniature works of art, but as means to an end. In other words, questions are about function rather than form. This is both humbling and liberating. It means that you must be prepared to admit that a question that you thought was beautifully crafted and certain to make a difference may, in fact, have created no movement at all in your client. But it also absolves you from the burden of having to think of each individual question as being more significant than it really is.

Questioning can also be a critical stance, as later described in Chapter 4. Choosing to ask, or not ask, a question can be a decision about whom to challenge and whom to keep safe. For example, we find that coaches are often hesitant to raise issues of equity because they are worried about the reaction of the other person, who could feel that they are being accused, at worst, of being racist and, at best, of not trying hard enough to advance the achievement of all students. And so having the perceived self-efficacy to engage with colleagues regarding issues of equity is vital for successful coaching. Chapter 4 offers further details on how coaches can use an equity lens while engaging in meaningful questioning.

Setting Goals

The job of the coach is to help others reach their goals, and those goals should also link to the larger goals, or strategy, of the organization. Specifically, goals are nested, and there must be a throughline that connects the smallest goal—what needs to be accomplished during the coaching conversation (e.g., develop a shared understanding of math instructional leadership)—with the largest organizational goal (e.g., improve students' STEM college and career readiness).

Despite the extent to which goals are centered in education reform, they are frequently misunderstood or misapplied. Our experience as coaches working with superintendents and principals tells us that goals are often assumed to be much more powerful than they actually are. Yes, in some ways it helps to set and work toward an ambitious goal, but that alone will not improve outcomes for students. The goal is not the mechanism that brings about improvement; instead, it is the work done to enhance the learning of students that improves outcomes for students.

In addition, coaches need to know what kind of goal will be helpful. Most goals required in school improvement and professional learning plans are performance goals, which set a numerical target. And when people already know how to do whatever is being measured, a performance goal can elicit the highest performance. But when people don't already know how to do what the goal measures, then trying to meet a performance goal elicits lower performance than simply asking people to do their best. This is because, when given a performance goal that they don't know how to meet, people tend to shift quickly from tactic to tactic in the hunt for the one that will get them closest to their goal (Earley et al., 1989).

When people don't already know how to do what the goal measures, they would be better off with a learning goal because it shifts attention toward the discovery and implementation of task-relevant strategies that, over time, result in higher performance (Seijts et al., 2004). Coaches can play an instrumental role in working with colleagues on setting and then reaching learning goals.

Providing Feedback

> Giving feedback seems to be the second most essential ingredient of life itself—after air, and before water. Humans can live for about three minutes without air, three days without water, and three months without food. But according to our observations, most people cannot live more than three hours without offering someone else an observation about themselves—often in the form of advice.
>
> —Seashore et al., 1992, p. 26

Of all the skills and activities we discuss in our coaching workshops, feedback is the one that is most misunderstood. When we, as coaches, work with educators on feedback, we typically begin by asking them to list what they know about the key features of good feedback. The responses most often include: timely, specific, actionable, constructive, concrete, and goal-oriented. We rarely get responses that go beyond these adjectives, and participants are often surprised by what we share: Feedback is not an unmitigated benefit to the receiver; more feedback is not always beneficial. The features of useful feedback go beyond its adjectives and extend to the mechanisms of feedback.

We find this lack of understanding of feedback alarming, especially if considering how much coaching and supervision (plus teaching!) are predicated on the notion that feedback is "a good thing," that educators know how to give constructive feedback, and that educators will be grateful for and responsive to feedback. Furthermore, feedback is enmeshed with multiple issues of equity. For example, teachers' low expectations of some students lead them to give feedback that they think those students can cope with. White supervisors tend to give less frank feedback to their direct reports who are people of color, perhaps because they are concerned about being thought of as racist.

Despite these nuances and pitfalls of feedback, many texts on coaching still treat it as a neutral, technical topic. We counter this by sharing that not all feedback is useful. Kluger and De Nisi (1996) conducted a meta-analysis of studies of feedback with the goal of better understanding the repeated finding that not all feedback leads to improved performance. They reviewed 131 research reports, determining that while, on average, feedback does improve performance, the effect sizes vary greatly, and 38% (231 out of 607) of the effect sizes they analyzed were negative. In other words, the feedback suppressed rather than improved the performance of the receiver. The finding that feedback is not always useful—and may even be harmful—should give us pause to reflect.

The second big challenge associated with feedback is that what really matters is the response that the feedback prompts in the receiver. Therefore, the coach should relinquish the idea that clarity, timeliness, and utility are sufficient in making feedback helpful; they also must consider multiple attributes of the feedback recipient.

Typically, we think of feedback as evaluative information or expert advice. The research on effective feedback suggests that feedback might be questions that encourage us to judge for ourselves whether we are clear on the goal, whether we can self-assess, and whether we know what to do next. We pay more attention to feedback that we generate for ourselves, and feedback questions that encourage self-regulation are intended to build capacity over the long term rather than sustain dependence on an outside expert. As such, we encourage coaching models to include feedback questioning.

Now that we, as coaches, know that educators will, when asked what good feedback looks like, typically fall back on assumptions based on old mental models, we ask a different question. We ask them to write about a time when feedback had a powerful impact on them. Those personal stories reveal a much more nuanced picture. People tell about episodes when someone they had never met before gave them feedback that was enormously helpful; when a close family member made a disparaging and disrespectful remark; when a professor made an encouraging suggestion that changed the direction of their lives; when a supervisor shared an opinion that they weren't ready for a leadership position. From sharing these stories, the workshop participants paint a much more colorful and sophisticated picture of feedback conversations.

Here, we list how not all feedback is equally useful and sometimes may actually be detrimental for both coachee and coach:

- Feedback that coachees perceive is about them personally is often counter-productive: Praise tends to communicate that they possess a quality that is valued; intimations that they don't measure up tend to elicit a defensive response.

- Feedback about the task tells the coachee what to do and is helpful when it clarifies the goal. For instance, "You need to speak more loudly; it was difficult to hear you" is helpful when the coachee didn't know that they couldn't be heard.

- Feedback about the process tells the coachee how to think about doing the task. For instance, "Plan the meeting using this template" is useful when it provides information that the coachee did not previously have, either about the goal or how to accomplish the goal.

- Feedback about self-regulation enables the coachee to be more metacognitive about their performance. For example, "What is your goal in having that meeting? How will you know whether the teachers benefited from that workshop?" helps coachees answer the feedback questions for themselves.

Finally, the most important feedback is the feedback coachees give themselves. Not surprisingly, if we receive feedback that does not accord with our own perceptions of what is good, we tend to reject it (Ivancevich & McMahon, 1982). For this reason, there are benefits when coaches advance their clients' own skills and strategies for reflection and self-evaluation. We articulate that leaders across levels of the education system should consider the time and other supports necessary so that coaches can listen, question, set goals, and deliver feedback to coachees to cultivate learning and foster equity.

TO MAKE COACHING MATTER

Concentrating on the craft of coaching, this chapter explained facets of bedrock coaching practices. We exposed ties between coaching and theory and research on adult learning and motivation. And we pointed to the need for infrastructure and leadership permitting coaches to carry out key activities in a caring, contextualized manner. In the following lists, we offer a gameplan for district leaders, principals, and coaches to more sharply focus on the craft of coaching. These recommendations for strengthening coaching are not a set-in-stone recipe, but are meant to spark reflection, discussion, and collaborative work. As coherence is necessary across levels of the education system, we share leadership moves for individuals in different roles. Further, we encourage clear, consistent, and open communication on who is doing what to make coaching matter.

District leaders should:

- clearly define the nature of high-leverage coaching practices, including questioning, listening, setting goals, and providing feedback;
- create positive organizational conditions so that coaches can carry out high-leverage coaching practices on a regular, routinized basis; and
- provide ongoing, contextualized learning opportunities to coaches on key coaching practices (e.g., questioning, setting goals) to continually improve their work.

Principals should:

- provide time and space for coaches to conduct key practices, including questioning, listening, setting goals, and providing feedback;
- communicate with teachers about how and why coaches will engage in questioning, listening, setting goals, and providing feedback; and
- use the practices of questioning, listening, setting goals, and providing feedback to mirror coaches' efforts with teachers.

Coaches should:

- use questioning, listening, and feedback strategies to promote learning and change;
- carefully consider the types of goals that they set with coaches; and
- reflect on strengths and weaknesses in how they provide feedback, and engage in questioning and listening.

This chapter illuminated features of key coaching strategies, interrogating how and why coaches should build relationships, question, listen, provide feedback, and set goals to advance strategic, equitable change. As such, Chapter 2 honed in on the daily, elbow-to-elbow work of coaches. In contrast, the next chapter zooms out to explain the history of coaching, including waves of policy promoting coaching. Chapter 3, therefore, tackles the question of how the education system landed on coaching, what policymakers and leaders seek to gain from coaching, and why practitioners, policymakers, and researchers have faith in coaching as an improvement lever.

The Why of Coaching

Our experience working with school district leaders to strengthen coaching tells us that, often, they are not entirely clear why their system adopted coaching, why coaches should undertake specific activities, and why coaching works. Returning to our topic of making coaching matter, we take several steps back to make clear why systems now rely on coaching, why state and district leaders have adopted coaching, and why coaching has the potential to promote learning and change across all levels. We ask and address these questions not to receive funny looks, nor to pontificate on historical trends, but, rather, to provide a clear foundation to strengthen coaching across settings to reach strategic, equitable goals. That is, although coaching is a popular reform instrument, which is deeply supported by policymakers and educators across numerous contexts, many leaders and teachers lack robust responses to the following questions: What needs does coaching fill? What problems does coaching address? How does coaching solve those issues? We argue it is vital to answer these questions to better zip together problems of educational reform with coaching as a solution. We must also address these questions to improve systems of support for coaches to meet lofty objectives.

This chapter provides historical background on coaching, including the rise of reading specialists in the 1980s–1990s and waves of education policy promoting coaching, and also explains underlying reasons for the adoption and spread of coaching. Next, we discuss why the education system leans on coaching as an improvement strategy. Our attempt to answer the deeper "why" of coaching is not merely an intellectual exercise, since unpacking the roots of—and rationales for—coaching is vital for leaders to create appropriate conditions for coaching and coaches to flourish. Finally, we encourage leaders to chart coaching in their specific contexts and share stances on their reasons for adopting—and investing in—coaching. By examining the history of coaching, leaders can better understand successes and pitfalls in coaches' work and educators' willingness to engage in coaching to reach strategic, equity-oriented goals.

Thus, this chapter advances the argument that, while coaching can be a powerful tool for change, in order to form logical links between strategy, equity, and coaching, educational leaders must gain awareness of why, how, and under what circumstances coaching operates to make a difference for teachers and schools.

WHY COACHING?

In the following, we grapple with three whys of coaching to help explain the role of coaching for strategic, equitable change and further explain each one throughout this chapter:

1. Why did coaching emerge?
   To understand the current nature of—and future directions for—coaching, educators, reformers, and researchers need to understand the historical roots of coaching. Educational policies promoted coaching, contributing to its skyrocketing popularity across settings. Further, these policies shape coaching in addition to coaches' work. We point to the layering of coaching's structures and practices over time, indicating that current forms of coaching are not necessarily intentionally designed.

2. Why do educational organizations adopt coaching?
   To address the question of why a range of districts and schools adopt coaching to achieve numerous objectives, we delve into the goals of coaching. In particular, we explain leaders' intentions for adopting coaching and what they believe their organization can gain through coaching. We consider why leaders choose coaching over other approaches to adult learning or organizational change. That is, what do leaders view as the on-the-ground advantages of coaching? And how do these benefits balance the high cost of coaching? This question is tied to the notion that leaders are always making choices, so selecting and prioritizing coaching means discontinuing, or saying no to, other investments. Additionally, we delve into why leaders believe coaching will drive improvement. That is, what is the rationale for an organization to place faith (and a host of resources) in coaching? We remind leaders to be transparent about their theory of action for coaching and inform others about the levers coaching can pull.

3. Why does coaching work?
   Finally, to help answer the question of why coaching works, we devote attention to the evidence base on the effectiveness of coaching. This incorporates points on how coaching functions as a tool for adult learning and organizational change.

In the following sections, we begin answering these three big-picture questions associated with coaching. We discuss the roots of coaching and implicit assumptions baked into coaching to ensure contemporary system and school leaders can improve the design and implementation of strategic, equity-centered coaching.

Why Did Coaching Emerge?

Coaching morphed into its current form through accident rather than design. This brief history shows how current models of coaching represent the accretion of different approaches to coaching over time. For this reason, it is necessary for reformers, leaders, coaches, and teachers to reflect on their experiences with different coaching models over time.

In contrast to many longstanding features of the education system (Cuban, 1990; Tyack & Cuban, 1995), including teachers, students, instructional materials, and testing, coaching is relatively new. Coaching was rare in the 1980s through the early 1990s (Bean et al., 2004; Dole, 2004; Domina et al., 2015). Prior to the 1980s, teachers and leaders gained knowledge and skills about their core tasks through educator preparation programs, received formal and informal mentorship in schools, and were generally released to enact their responsibilities as they saw fit. During this period, district and school leaders were less attentive to issues of instructional leadership and coherence (Hallinger, 2005; Rigby, 2014). In some contexts, principals and teacher mentors attempted to support teachers in an individualized manner. Yet, the notion of systemic reform, or system-wide instructional improvement through coaching or other modes of teacher support, was not yet established.

Coaching gained steam as systemic and accountability reforms ascended in the U.S. education system (Dole, 2004; Smith & O'Day, 1990). Coaching filled an important need as teaching shifted from private work inside a classroom to publicly accountable work under No Child Left Behind (NCLB), state, and district policy. Coaching became a lever for enacting change to the technical core of schooling: teaching and learning.

Coaching impels these changes by operating in a counternormative manner and, as a consequence, coaches' work plays a role in changing the norms of teaching itself (Little, 1982; Lortie, 2002). Here, we explicitly refer to how coaching breaks down Lortie's (2002) norms of teaching: individualism, privatism, and conservatism. Table 3.1 offers examples of how coaching runs counter to Lortie's (2002) norms of teaching. This is due to coaches' efforts in shifting norms of teaching when they enter classrooms to observe instruction, or meet with groups of teachers together, and guide teachers to make changes to instruction. Simply stated, a coach is an extra educator, an additional presence with an additional set of eyes, ears, and hands, thus preventing a teacher from working in isolation or alone as an individual.

Table 3.1. How coaching disrupts three norms of the teaching profession.

Norm of Teaching	How Coaching Disrupts the Norm	Example
Individualism: Teachers work individually inside their classroom	Coaches partner with educators, reducing the isolation of teachers inside their classrooms	A coach co-teaches an NGSS-aligned science lesson with a teacher
Conservatism: Teachers maintain previous practices	Coaches encourage new thinking and ways of doing school	A coach works with a team of 3rd-grade teachers to encourage them to adopt new pedagogical routines in their writing instruction
Presentism: Teachers respond to immediate needs and challenges	Coaches enable long-term visioning and planning	A coach works with a middle school teacher to create a long-term plan for math instruction

Further, when coaches work alongside teachers, they diminish the norm of privatism (Lortie, 2002). That is, coaches reduce educators' privacy in carrying out their work through elbow-to-elbow coaching routines. Finally, by concentrating on motivating change, coaching dismantles the norm of conservatism (Coburn & Woulfin, 2012; Woulfin, 2018). Coaches transmit new ideas about teaching and leading, and work alongside educators to promote strategic, equitable change in the classroom and school. Therefore, coaching catalyzes change, rather than conserving older activities. In sum, coaching represents a challenge to the status quo of teaching plus schooling. Based upon this, it is vital to properly support educators' understandings of the benefits of discarding (or at least softening) long-standing norms of schooling so that coaching can thrive.

Standards Movement. The standards movement of the late 1990s shifted attention toward consistent, coherent forms of teacher support so that all teachers might teach standards-aligned curriculum (Smith & O'Day, 1990). U.S. schools became more and more focused on standards-based instruction, in which teachers were expected to use standards-based curriculum to raise student achievement as measured by standards-based standardized tests. This placed pressure on teachers to conduct instruction in new ways. This also directed attention to both the processes (e.g., curriculum implementation, nature of instruction) as well as outcomes of instruction (e.g., student test scores). As such, leaders gained the ability to peer into the black box of teaching and learning. Stemming from this, district and state leaders began creating a new, middle-level position, with the label of coach. We posit they adopted the coach term to capture the stance toward improvement, learning, growth, development, and change—without the "teeth" or authority of a supervisor or manager (Campbell & van Nieuwerburgh, 2017).

By the late 1990s, educational reformers and leaders were heavily invested in the nature of instruction, standardization of practice, and coherence across grade levels and schools. They applied the theory of action that if schools were held accountable for instruction and student outcomes, the quality of teaching would increase and student learning would improve (Anagnostopoulos, 2003; Smith & O'Day, 1990). Across states and districts, accountability systems and research pulled back the curtain on gaps in achievement and, at times, instructional quality. Subsequently, states adopted new standards and curricular materials that asked teachers to teach and lead in new, and often highly specified, ways (Kersten & Pardo, 2007; Rowan & Correnti, 2009). In many contexts, leaders expanded and refined professional learning opportunities to build teachers' capacity on standards-based instruction in an attempt to reach high targets on standardized tests (Hochberg & Desimone, 2010). Amidst these large-scale changes in educational policy and practice, state and district administrators gained awareness that principals were already overburdened, so someone else was needed to help with the work of improving instruction and outcomes. Thus, administrators turned to coaching, and the creation of the coach role, to improve outcomes in a manner matching these accountability-oriented, standards-based reforms.

While working toward accountability-oriented goals, policymakers and administrators also allocated funding for systemic reform and to increase coherence; this permitted hiring and supporting coaches (Domina et al., 2015; Knight, 2012). We trace major policy movements in the timeline shown in Figure 3.1. During this period, underperforming districts and schools, often in underserved communities with high concentrations of students of color, were prioritized to apply for additional funds in support of coaching.

Figure 3.1. A timeline of coaching since the 1980s.

1980s	1990s	2000s	2010s	2020–beyond
Mentor teachers; Reading specialists	Title I improvement coaches	Reading First coaches; Curriculum coaches	Common Core curriculum coaches; Data coaches; Equity coaches; Leadership coaches	Educator support coaches

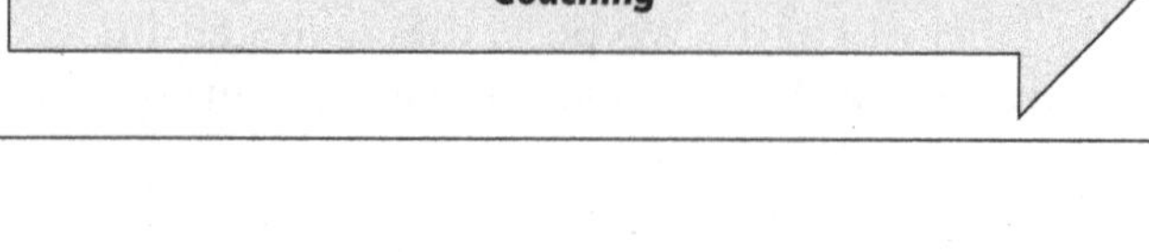

Coaching

To further explain shifts in education policy that shaped the nature of coaching and continue to influence the design of coaching systems and the nature of coaches' work, we provide details on two federal accountability policies: Reading First and Race to the Top. Reading First popularized a form of reading coaching, and Race to the Top advanced data-based decision-making, with coaches facilitating data use alongside teachers and principals.

Reading First

The Reading First program, a branch of NCLB, concentrated on changing the nature of K–3 reading instruction and literacy outcomes (Deussen et al., 2007). Reading First played a major role in boosting coaching across the United States. By 2004, most states were implementing Reading First, and this included hiring and relying on coaches to promote particular forms of reading instruction and supporting teachers in using specific instructional materials and assessments (Haager et al., 2008). Evaluations of Reading First showed that schools with a high level of Reading First implementation and coaching had higher student achievement compared with control schools (Haager et al., 2008). Other research on Reading First coaching revealed how coaches engaged with teachers and encouraged the adoption of Reading First–aligned instructional materials, pedagogical routines, and data analysis meetings (Coburn & Woulfin, 2012; Kersten & Pardo, 2007). These results quantified and advertised the potential of coaching to advance school reform.

For our purposes, however, it is more important to foreground the way Reading First taught leaders and teachers about coaching itself. That is, during the early to mid-2000s, Reading First initiated coaching in many contexts. Thus, this policy provided many teachers with their first experiences being coached, and it promoted many educators into the coach role. It is probable that, currently, many district leaders', principals', and teachers' first coaches held the title of Reading First coach. Consequently, many educators' vision of coaching looks like the coaching from Reading First coaches. We posit, therefore, Reading First shaped how teachers, coaches, and other leaders conceive of coaching. In fact, one of us served as a Reading First reading coach, and we are curious how many readers worked as a Reading First coach or experienced coaching from one!

Finally, the roots and shoots of Reading First helped proliferate myriad coaching models. For instance, some districts developed math coaching models mirroring the Reading First coaching model. These districts designed systems for math coaches to advance the implementation of specific math instructional materials, observe and provide feedback on math instruction, and analyze students' math achievement data. We also suggest that this lineage from Reading First coaches to math and then science coaches, extends to leadership and equity coaches. Chapter 8 provides greater detail on these varieties of coaching as well as how to ensure infrastructure sustains various models of coaching.

Race to the Top

As the accountability policy era marched along, coaches continued playing a key role in reform efforts. Race to the Top (RTT) was funded in 2009 and invited states to create plans incorporating policies including new standards, school turnaround initiatives, and educator evaluation systems. States competed for funding by proposing procedures for evaluating teachers with more teeth than before (Steinberg & Donaldson, 2016). Coaches, lacking the authority of administrators (and frequently not wanting this authority) are typically divorced from evaluation (Galey-Horn & Woulfin, 2021). Nevertheless, RTT spotlighted the nature of instruction, issues of teacher quality, and how principals could provide targeted support and professional development to teachers (Gabriel & Woulfin, 2017). In response, some district and school leaders did elect to weave evaluation with coaching in particular ways (Galey-Horn & Woulfin, 2021). For example, some coaches provided PD on aspects of the evaluation rubric to help teachers clearly understand facets of the framework for high-quality teaching as enumerated by the evaluation rubric.

During this period, many districts began assigning coaches to turnaround schools, and some offered district-based turnaround coaching to principals. These coaches were expected to motivate specific changes aligning to turnaround reform. For example, coaches facilitated data analysis meetings and led PD on instructional approaches delineated by turnaround reform (Trujillo & Woulfin, 2014; Weiner & Woulfin, 2018). Therefore, turnaround policy provided resources bolstering coaching, while coaches were tasked with advancing turnaround reform. Moreover, turnaround coaching models leaned on the notion that underserved schools and underperforming teachers should be the primary focus of coaches. This emphasis on coaching to significantly improve schools and teaching makes sense in some regards, but it could contribute to negative perceptions of coaching (e.g., schools with coaches are "failing," educators with coaches are "in trouble"). It could also contribute to educators perceiving coaching as a punishment instead of as a beneficial tool, or asset, enabling ongoing learning to support reaching locally generated goals.

Although a variety of models and forms of coaching arose in the 2010s, the financial crisis and state- and district-level budget cuts resulted in some districts reducing the number of coach positions and changing the structure of their coaching model. In particular, this entailed shifting from school-based coaching to a districtwide coaching model to stretch resources. These budget issues elevate the necessity of maximizing coaching to attain its full potential in light of its large price tag.

Leadership Coaching. During these waves of reform, many districts began using coaching to develop and support their principals, otherwise known as leadership coaching. This is partially because district administrators noticed gaps in the preparation of school leaders, the too-muchness of the principalship, and the high bar of next-generation accountability policy. It made sense to institute leadership coaching to fill these gaps and boost principals' capacity along multiple dimensions.

Leadership coaching borrows tenets from instructional coaching, such as providing contextualized, just-in-time support; modeling; and supporting reflection. Some research indicates principal coaching can increase leadership skills (Bickman et al., 2012), but there appears to be a wide range of approaches to leadership coaching. Notably, many large urban districts shifted the principal supervisors' role to embrace a coaching stance, and district administrators adopted expectations that supervisors would conduct coaching activities with their principals (Goldring et al., 2018; Saltzman, 2016). While partnering with principal supervisors, we have noticed common coaching activities to include: supervisor–principal walkthroughs and debrief conversations, reflecting on data trends in the school, co-developing school improvement plans, and texting about how to resolve an issue with special education services or school operations. Thus, leadership coaching can address many elements of schooling, rely on many forms of evidence on teaching and learning, and involve many types of communication.

Why Do Organizations Adopt Coaching?

Depending on policy guidance, accountability pressures, and local resources and factors, districts and schools adopt coaching for numerous reasons. Reformers and leaders clearly adopt coaching to fix different problems and satisfy different needs. Even within a single context, we have seen leaders enact coaching to address several needs. Some district leaders may view coaching as helping to achieve lofty goals for teaching reforms and leading and improving outcomes. Other district leaders may view coaching as a strategy to support principals and retain teachers. Some school leaders may view coaching as lightening the load of instructional leadership by developing and supporting teachers on their behalf. Other school leaders may deem coaching as a tool for maintaining compliance with district initiatives. Based upon these variable conceptions of coaching, some coaches may view the coach role as a way to mentor teachers and leaders, improve instruction/leadership, or advance particular initiatives. Other coaches may view the coach role as a professional step on the career ladder from teacher to leader.

Although we are huge fans of coaching and advocates of deploying coaching, we will point out that sometimes a decision to hire coaches, or to use coaching to address a particular problem, is itself a product of "solutionitis." Coaching is expensive because it is labor-intensive, and it entails hiring relatively highly paid employees. Experienced teachers, as opposed to new teachers, are hired as coaches, and they earn higher salaries. Coaching is also inefficient because a coach can only work with a limited number of individuals or small groups per day and week.

And even if there were infinite resources and coaches, it may be possible that certain issues are not fixable through coaching. For example, we have known a literacy director who expected coaches to "fix" the problem that teachers were not using the newly adopted instructional materials. The literacy director assumed that the teachers did not know how to use the new materials or were "resistant to change." The literacy director also detected many coaches who were not engaged in curriculum-focused coaching. But with a little digging, we discovered that principals in this district had redirected funds to purchase other materials, so teachers continued using other materials, including the previous literacy program. The literacy director, then, had to accept that, to the extent that there was a problem, it was of her own creation. The director then realized that there were many parts about the literacy program and its budget that she had failed to communicate to teachers and principals.

Thus, when superintendents and principals bring up coaching as a solution for any given problem, we first ask questions such as: "Why did your district adopt coaching?"; and "Why do you believe coaching will work?" But we also ask: "If you didn't have coaches, what would you do to reach current goals?" and "If you couldn't afford coaching, what alternatives are you considering?" Leaders can save a lot of time and money investigating the problem before creating solutions, and often the problem they have at the end of this process is not the problem they initially thought.

To answer our second question on why educational organizations, and their leaders, adopt coaching, we return to the theory of action of coaching: If systems adopt coaching, coaches will serve as leaders who build capacity and promote change, and other educators will learn more about how to work effectively toward strategic, equitable goals. Therefore, coaching is a system-level professional learning model aiming to motivate change. Figure 3.2 shows five interrelated mechanisms by which coaching fulfills its theory of action and, ultimately, reaches its target:

1. Build capacity
2. Foster coherence
3. Strengthen networks
4. Elevate the profession
5. Promote strategic, equitable change

Figure 3.2. Coaching fulfills its theory of action through five interrelated mechanisms.

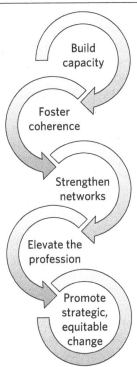

First, coaching builds capacity so all educators continually learn and so the system can meet challenging goals (Gibbons et al., 2017; Matsumura et al., 2013). In this way, coaching stands on the premise that each and every educator can—and should—learn, change, and improve. Coaching also assumes that, due to shifting pressures and foci in the education system—including new waves of reform with new expectations for teaching, leading, and numerous components of schooling—educators must continually learn. That is, it is neither realistic nor sufficient to rely on educator preparation programs or individualistic forms of mentoring to build teacher capacity. Instead, a systemic approach to professional learning, via coaching, is vital.

By providing ongoing, contextualized, elbow-to-elbow learning opportunities, coaching builds capacity. Indeed, coaching varies from bite-sized, just-in-time support to teachers and leaders to guiding the thinking and planning of expert educators. For instance, a coach–teacher conversation in the hallway after a professional development session and a coach's written feedback after observing a principal-led instructional leadership team meeting both constitute learning opportunities that build capacity.

Second, coaching fosters coherent, continuous improvement by creating a position that looks across the educational organization, collecting and analyzing evidence on what is working for whom under what conditions. In Chapter 7, we provide details on how to engage in such continuous improvement activities. As boundary spanners, coaches are well positioned to detect the degree of organizational coherence, such as when teachers use vastly different discourse and engagement strategies or when leaders provide vastly different forms of feedback after classroom walkthroughs. Further, the coach role is well suited to encourage common ways of teaching and leading across a school or district. Coaches can spread key ideas tied to strategy and equity to educators across contexts. Coaches can also wield informal authority to persuade others to adopt new ideas, or at least try them out (Woulfin, 2015). And they can do so in a way that builds coherence because the coach is able to be an agent of consistency. Yet, for this to unfold, leaders must build coaches' capacity so that they are well prepared to deliver common messages and learning opportunities on reform and, through this, raise coherence.

Third, coaching strengthens networks because coaches forge links with educators in different roles, sites, and across levels of the education system. For example, a leadership coach creates ties with multiple principals, enabling ideas, information, and other resources to flow across the set of leaders. Coaches can draw upon their knowledge of other educators' strengths and needs, bringing together teams of educators to collaborate and learn as a community. Within districts, we have observed how coaches connect educators, permitting the cross-pollination of ideas across classrooms and sites, to enable learning and change.

Fourth, by uplifting educators, coaching boosts professionalism regarding teaching and leading. Notably, when district- and school-based coaches offer contextualized professional learning opportunities, they support the education profession from an insider stance. That is, coaches' solutions elevate the knowledge and skills of insiders, using localized knowledge to meet the needs of the specific context. Further, as it hinges on notions of continuous improvement, coaching advances the norm of professionalism. More specifically, coaching promotes professionalism through its premise that all educators can develop capacity through observation, reflection, and modeling.

Fifth, coaching advances equitable change in and through learning. In this book, we concentrate on coaching as a lever for carrying out strategic, equity-oriented change. Thus, we highlight how coaching uses targeted, tailored learning opportunities to systematically motivate deep levels of change to the technical core of schools: teaching and leading. Coaching elevates the premise that change happens in and through adult and organizational learning, rather than through a reliance on the rules of accountability systems or the carrots-and-sticks of incentive systems. We also highlight that coaching has the potential to work toward strategic, equity-oriented change when structures, conditions, and leadership are aligned to enable coaches to do their best work. Indeed, coaching is optimized by creating and refining structures and systems for strategic, equity-centered coaching.

Equity and Coaching. Indicating an awareness of both the barriers for reaching challenging, equity-centered goals and the catalytic power of coaching to substantively alter teaching and leading, coaching has also been adopted to help educators, and the wider education system, work in more equitable ways. Leaders perceive that coaching plays a vital role in supporting teachers and leaders to reach strategic, equitable goals. As discussed in Chapter 4, coaching has been woven with ambitious, equity-oriented school reforms. In particular, coaching can develop the knowledge, skills, and dispositions of teachers and leaders around equity issues, including culturally responsive classroom discourse and equitable approaches to discipline (Aguilar, 2020). Moreover, a coaching model can be designed so coaches purposefully direct attention toward equitable, anti-racist, and inclusive models of teaching and learning (Orange et al., 2019). Integrating coaching and equity can help reshape the nature of a wide range of structures and practices, including culturally sustaining instruction, parent engagement, detracking reforms, and special education services.

As discussed throughout this book, coaching has functioned as a multipurpose tool—over different time periods, for various systems, and among different actors. But system leaders should not haphazardly adopt coaching, as it can serve competing purposes and work toward numerous targets. Rather, the purposes and targets of coaching must connect with the educational organization's pressing problems and strategic objectives. Many times, these purposes are obscured or downplayed to teachers, leaders, and even coaches! It is necessary to bring attention to each of these purposes—to promote coaching and, perhaps more importantly, to enable coaches to fulfill key goals. Throughout this book, we articulate how to connect these dots by aligning coaching with strategy to catalyze change and reach equitable outcomes.

How Coaching Functions for Change

In this section, we tackle the question of how coaching advances strategic, equitable change. Due to our passion regarding the ecosystem and conditions for coaching to matter, we not only address the reasons coaching "works" at the one-on-one, or cognitive, level. Instead, as shown by Figure 3.3, we address how coaching functions across multiple levels with schools: macro, meso, and micro. Applying concepts from organizational theory aids in explaining how coaching works toward improvement across multiple levels.

Figure 3.3. How coaching functions across three organizational levels.

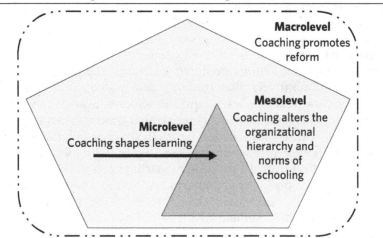

We begin by describing how coaching functions from the macrolevel orientation. Paired with state and district policies and leaders, coaches are nested in a complex field with educators, leaders, parents, community-based organizations, and professional development (PD) providers (Rowan, 2002; Trujillo & Woulfin, 2014). Coaches often see and hear the "big picture" of educational reform—whether state policy shifts or district priorities. At the macrolevel, different players in the educational reform field may advance different ideas about both coaching and instruction. For instance, state administrators may advance sets of ideas about mathematics instruction, but district leaders may communicate other ideas on mathematics assessment. Coaches can enmesh these ideas in their work and, in turn, couple these ideas into school-level changes (Coburn & Woulfin, 2012; Woulfin, 2016). In turn, a mathematics coach based in a school would interpret different messages from different levels and then incorporate them into their daily work. Thus, a coach is a leader who interprets and frames messages about initiatives or programs to motivate equitable change (Coburn, 2006; Woulfin, 2015). More importantly, coaching is effective when a coach teaches their client about the strategy, or the model for teaching or leading. Based upon this, crystallizing the major improvement strategy is vital, and coaches' communication skills to broadcast the strategy is paramount. That is, the clarity of the strategic plan matters so the coach can make sense of key messages and then effectively, persuasively broadcast those messages to different people across contexts.

Second, from a meso-level stance, coaching contributes to change by altering structures, routines, and practices in an organization to meet goals. Interestingly, coaches often carve out a new level in the organization chart, such as between the superintendent and principals, or between the academic director and EL specialists, or between the principal and teachers.

The organizational position of coaches shapes their work. In many instances, coaches mention being "in the middle" or working "on their own island." And, conceptually, coaches are intermediaries who are sandwiched between organizational actors of differing power and authority (Kane & Rosenquist, 2019). Instructional coaches, for example, are sandwiched between teachers and district leaders. Based upon their position in the organization chart, coaches can be deployed to transmit ideas and information up, down, or along the organization. Returning to the example of an instructional coach, they deliver information with teachers, but also communicate ideas to principals and district administrators as well as other coaches.

In addition, meso-lenses remind us to consider how coaches' work is influenced in multiple ways by organizational conditions, including the school calendar and schedule, layout of the school building and meeting facilities, and norms regarding collaboration and transparency (Shirrell & Spillane, 2020). Coaches create ties among teachers and leaders to foster learning and change. In particular, coaches serve as matchmakers who facilitate educators in learning from each other's strengths. Notably, coaches hold insights as to the strengths of other teachers in the building. And coaches facilitate team discussions and activities to ensure ideas flow across ties (Woulfin, 2018). In addition, coaches can encourage teams to focus on certain areas and learn from certain educators' practices (Coburn & Woulfin, 2012; Galey-Horn & Woulfin, 2021). In sum, coaches function as a broker among people and ideas.

At the micro-level, coaches engage with educators to build capacity; we discuss several coaching moves in Chapter 2. At the micro-level, coaching is a conversation between two or more educators with the intent of improving the practice of at least one of them. This conversation typically involves the intentional application of coaching skills by a coach who provides a space for others to think about their challenges, assumptions, options, and next steps. By asking questions, injecting new information, and providing feedback, the coach provides scaffolding for the coachee's thinking process. Further, the coach provides encouragement and soft accountability by expressing faith in what others can do and asking them to commit to trying something and then following up.

We are keenly aware of the microprocesses of coaching occurring not only in organizations but within the minds of people, so we also devote attention to the psychology of coaching. Guided by the notion that meaningful change occurs through substantive learning, we consider how the learning of an educator, or specifically a coachee, is motivated and accelerated by positive dispositions toward the coach and coaching and the enactment of supportive, reflective routines. First, many educators have positive associations with the coach or coaching term; this enables a certain level of openness to and for coaching.

Second, and perhaps more importantly, coaching hinges on motivating adult learners through supportive, contextualized practice and reflection. In particular, as described in Chapter 2, a skillful coach finds ways to encourage the coachee to take new steps, attempt new practices, and think in new ways about an issue and their work. We propose that, through these encouraging routines, coaches motivate change aligned to the strategy.

TO MAKE COACHING MATTER

This chapter turned back the clock—and pulled back the curtain—on how coaching became a well-regarded instrument for educational improvement. In the following recommendations, we describe steps district leaders, principals, and coaches can take to develop educators' knowledge about the why of coaching as well as to align structures and practices to enable reform-oriented coaching. These concrete leadership moves, attending to the policy context and organizational norms, can help make coaching matter.

District leaders should:

- document, analyze, and reflect on the policies, guidelines, norms, and resources associated with coaching;
- document the history of coaching in their context;
- communicate with leaders and teachers how coaching aligns with current policies as well as previous reform efforts; and
- develop coaches' understanding of their roles and responsibilities spanning the macro-, meso-, and microlevels.

Principals should:

- understand how coaching relates to past and present policies or initiatives;
- clarify to teachers how coaches' work will tie to specific policies, reforms, and/or initiatives;
- clarify to teachers the deeper rationale for engaging in coaching; and
- communicate with coaches about major goals for the school related to current reforms/initiatives.

Coaches should:

- understand the policy landscape, including key features of current system and school reforms;

- reflect on how their work addresses multiple purposes of coaching; and
- develop teachers' understanding of the deeper rationale for coaching as well as features of the current coaching model and its associated activities.

Chapter 3 demystified the origin and complexity of coaching, and it described the centrality of coaching in multiple educational reforms. We trace how accountability policies adopted coaching and relied on coaches to carry ideas and implement practices. Strikingly, many of these policies made nods to access, equality, and equity, yet they left many children, communities, and educators (including coaches) behind. In the next chapter, we confront these disconnects between saying equity and engaging in equity work. Specifically, Chapter 4 presents how to center equity in the structures, conceptualizations, and practices of coaching. This includes depicting how coaches can engage in equity-centered coaching routines that apply an equity lens. Chapter 4 also explains how leaders construct and promote conditions for coherent—and strategic—equity-centered coaching. Throughout, we assert that, for coaching to matter, infrastructure and leadership for coaching, in addition to coaches' daily work, must not only shine light on inequities but continually work toward equity-oriented goals for schools and society.

Centering Equity in Coaching

For there is always light, if only we're brave enough to see it, if only we're brave enough to be it.

—Amanda Gorman

Whether scanning newspaper headlines, watching the nightly news, or scrolling through Twitter, it is nearly impossible to not encounter reports of inequity, beginning with graphs showing disparities in academic achievement, disproportionalities in discipline referrals and graduation rates in schools, followed closely by income disparities across racial and gender groups, unemployment rates, access to healthcare, and police violence. Research broadcasting the "COVID slide" (oftentimes referred to with the deficit-based term "learning loss") calculates increasingly larger gaps between Black and Brown students and White students after several years of disrupted schooling (Goldhaber et al., 2022).

With education as one key to unlock children's potential for employment and overall wellness, it is clear that achieving educational equity matters if we are to create a more equitable society. Yet there remain significant, undeniable patterns in our schools as to who is being left behind; these patterns have lifelong implications affecting the degree to which one can access and enjoy full participation in our society. We articulate coaching is one policy instrument with the potential to make schools more equitable. This is because the structures of coaching and the daily work of coaches can—and should—serve to disrupt the aforementioned patterns in who is left behind by the education system. In this chapter, we explore the intersection of coaching and equity by portraying the goals, strategies, and practices of equity-centered coaching and explaining the structures of and conditions for equity-centered coaching to take place.

For our author team, equity and social justice are central in our professional as well as personal lives, and we are aware of the heightened attention to racism and inequity—ranging from Black Lives Matter and new forms of disability activism to mischaracterizations of Critical Race Theory and attempts to ban books on gender identity (Ray, 2022). We are struck by the current degree of political polarization—at this social and political moment, the mere mention of the word equity may be construed as divisive, adding another layer of difficulty to the essential work of improving access, opportunities, experiences, and outcomes for historically marginalized students. However, educational organizations across the United States use the equity term, and educators are driving toward equity in their work; therefore, we illuminate how coaching can unite educators, enabling districts and schools to reach equity-oriented goals.

Prior to delving into educational equity and depicting coaching activities that center equity in substantial ways, we highlight a few guiding principles on equity for coaches to implement. First, equity cannot advance sufficiently through a statement, an announcement, or an event. Rather, equity should be promoted through ongoing adult and organizational learning since it requires deep changes in norms, dispositions, systems, routines, communication, and practices. Second, equity cannot be siloed into one district department, or be the responsibility of a single district or school leader. Instead, equity should flow in and across departments, initiatives, people, and places. Third, equity-centered work should occur across all levels of the education system—from federal and state policies and funding priorities to the superintendent and chief academic officer, to the principal, coach, teachers, and staff (Irby et al., 2022). Again, these actors should be doing equity-focused work to help disrupt pervasive patterns in which certain students with certain identities and privileges attain particular educational outcomes. Fourth, and stemming from the prior principles, coaching can and should center equity, and coaches can and should support efforts to reach equity-oriented goals.

OUR DEFINITION OF EDUCATIONAL EQUITY

Equity is a broad term that carries multiple meanings and is applied in multiple ways. As we described, many definitions of equity distinguish it from notions of equality and access. We draw on the National Equity Project's definition: *Educational equity means that each child receives what they need to develop to their full academic and social potential.* Additionally, we take the stance that reaching equity in education involves transforming institutions and systems with the major goal of disrupting the connection between a student's racial, economic, (dis)ability, cultural, or other marginalized identity, and student outcomes.

So, let's be clear—when we talk about equity, we mean that students' opportunities, experiences, and outcomes should not be predicted by gender, race, ethnicity, class, or ability. This requires the elimination of inequities that contribute to disparate learning and achievement by students of differing social groups, and a critical examination of the normalized practices in education that discriminate against our most marginalized students. This includes eliminating inequities in instructional quality across different zip codes. We have seen how strategic plans, school schedules, instructional materials, writing instruction, and exposure to science and music instruction vary on different sides of the highway. These differences are rooted in inequity and contribute to additional inequities. We have also seen vastly different approaches to leadership, professional development, and coaching in different zip codes; they were institutionalized via inequity and reproduce inequity.

Finally, we treat equity work as requiring a thorough and thoughtful examination of the cognitive biases that have developed as a result of personal and professional socialization and how those biases influence the enactment of organizational routines. For example, educators must intentionally examine how racialized biases shape the ways they lead, teach, coach, and engage with families, staff, students, and others. Additionally, equity work requires an ongoing commitment to adult and organizational learning with a specific focus on deeply changing normalized practices, dispositions, systems, and routines that are often perceived as neutral yet ultimately contribute to the cumulative advantages experienced by some student groups, while disproportionately disadvantaging others (Lewis & Diamond, 2015). Finally, there must be an ongoing commitment to examining the results of changes to assess whether changes are truly making a difference in the access, opportunities, experiences, and outcomes for our most vulnerable and marginalized students.

FROM SAYING EQUITY TO WORKING FOR EQUITY

The concept of equity versus equality has been represented in a multitude of ways, including the oft-circulated image of three brown-skinned individuals, each a different height, standing at a fence watching a baseball game. One half of the picture is intended to represent equality, with each individual given the same intervention—a single crate on which to stand. It is clear in the picture that the intervention was unnecessary for the tallest individual but insufficient for the shortest. This points to the way that when everyone gets the same thing, it doesn't always "level the playing field." That is, equality is not fair; it is unjust. The other half of the picture is meant to represent equity, with each person receiving what they need to be able to see over the fence. The tallest person stands without a crate and has an uninterrupted view of the game, the medium-height individual stands on one crate, allowing a decent view of the game, and the shortest individual stands on two crates, finally able to see over the fence.

Although this picture is both problematic and overly simplistic in the way it represents the problem and potential solution, it does show how providing everyone the same intervention does not lead to an equitable outcome. But it also creates a lot of confusion: Does achieving equity mean taking something away from someone and giving it to someone else in order to give that person an advantage? Does the graphic problematize the height of the third individual rather than the fence? What does equity actually mean as it is represented in the graphic? How you see the problem determines *who* you see as the problem (Kendi, 2019). This is a reminder that, when centering equity, we should accurately represent the problem and carefully view the system that produced it.

These debates on the equity/equality picture illustrate numerous ways to conceive of equity, making it essential for educational organizations to have a shared understanding of what is meant by equity and what must be done to achieve it. Many districts have drafted equity statements as one step to form shared understandings and framing for equity. Powerful equity statements spotlight identity groups who are disproportionately represented in data as underperforming, acknowledge the structural and institutional conditions that lead to underperformance, and declare a commitment to create equitable access, opportunities, experiences, and outcomes for all students regardless of their social identity group.

Moreover, powerful equity statements not only define equity, but they outline necessary actions that commit the entire organization to the achievement of equity. For example, District C declared in formal district policy documents that, among other actions, they will achieve their definition of equity by "build(ing) awareness, capacity and consciousness through equity-focused professional learning to challenge and change the status quo," as well as "provid(ing) equitable resources in addition to culturally relevant and rigorous curriculum." In this example, critical reflection coupled with building knowledge and capacity about systemic oppression to change outcomes for students are proposed as levers for equitable change. Additionally, this example notes that allocating resources and shifting teacher practices are necessary to make change toward equity. Finally, the superintendent has been strategic in their use of the statement. This includes asking teachers, principals, and central office administrators to read the document before engaging in school or district work, issuing a reminder that whatever their work, it is centered in equity.

Of course, equity statements, similar to shiny strategy documents, are insufficient on their own because equity is not simply a declaration to be made, it is work that must be done. Actions are crucial for effecting change. And these actions must occur in an ongoing, routinized manner. As previously mentioned, equity work cannot be siloed; it must permeate every level of the organization. We note that equity-centered coaching, not just for teachers but also for school and district leaders, becomes much more accessible when equity has been deemed a north star by the superintendent and the school board.

Making equity central to the mission and strategic priorities of an educational organization communicates commitment to equity. It also helps create a shared understanding of equity-centered coaching among all individuals that efforts to achieve equity will not be a stand-alone event taken on by a superhero coach, divorced from the work of teaching and learning, but rather embraced by the entire school community as a capacity-building lever for improvement. When equity is central to the mission of the entire organization, coaches are better positioned to center equity within their work and build the capacity of the organization to deliver on the promise of *all*. Additionally, when the structures, routines, and practices of coaching center equity, it matters even more for learning and change to reach vital goals for society as well as schools. Providing a foundation for the routines and practices of equity-centered coaching, we next explain why and how to apply an equity lens in the context of coaching.

USING AN EQUITY LENS IN COACHING

We see coaching as existing in support of a district's vision for *all* students. This requires ensuring that, as educators engage in work aligned to the district or school improvement strategy, there are deliberate examinations of the impact of that strategy for students across identity groups. That deliberate examination is often described as using an equity lens. So, we declare that the application of an equity lens allows educators to view variation in access and opportunities afforded to students and adults based upon social identity group membership, ultimately leading to disparities in experiences and outcomes. If we add the application of an equity lens to the core work of a coach in asking questions and providing feedback, this positions coaches to facilitate intentional reflection with coachees to root out subtle, as well as glaring, inequities present across the educational sphere. Simply put, an equity lens can make visible inherent inequities across a system by looking beyond the written policies and procedures, and interrogating their impacts across race, ethnicity, gender, class, ableism, and home language (Ray, 2022).

An equity lens is based upon a set of core beliefs, assumptions, or perceptions that assist in understanding inequities that result from varied levels of oppression (National Equity Project). This lens typically asks the examiner to make determinations about access, opportunities, experiences, and outcomes across multiple identity groups with regards to equity. For example, in a classroom, an equity lens applied to an observation of a class discussion might incorporate questions, such as:

- How many times have you called on students who present as males versus students who present as female?

- Did your wait time for student responses vary depending upon the racial identity of the student?
- How did emergent bilingual students respond to the final question?

Essential to developing an equity lens is a close and critical examination of one's socialized worldview—how you have been brought up in society to view and value people across identity groups. None of us is immune to the messaging from family, friends, institutions, and media that signal the value and status of identity groups based on skin color, economic status, home language, (dis)ability, and gender orientation, to name a few. In fact, research tells us that we cannot be objective, or independent, of our socialization (Sensoy & DiAngelo, 2017). Therefore, the decisions educators make about who gets to participate in class, who gets to speak first in a meeting, or who gets to make a leadership error and try again, is filtered through our biases, and through the stereotypes that we hold about the capabilities of certain groups over others. Without interruption or interrogation, it is highly likely that biases reinforce the normalized, institutional practices that accompany teaching and leading, and so the perpetuation of inequities persists.

The application of an equity lens, across all aspects of schooling, and across the individual, interpersonal, and institutional levels, requires critical self-examination, skill building, practice, and feedback. For coaches, this should become a part of their practice; just as we expect that a coach has the requisite skills to listen, question, and provide feedback to coachees, so, too, should we expect coaches to have language, knowledge, and skills for using the equity lens.

Districts and schools have recently begun adopting protocols to guide the usage of the equity lens—a list of questions that they apply, for example, to decisions being made, policies being developed, and curriculum being reviewed or written. In one example, the Center for Urban Education (2015) created a list of questions based upon the following indicators:

1. Equity mindedness as a guiding paradigm
2. Equity in language
3. Data collection and reporting strategy
4. Disproportionate impact
5. Consistency and ubiquity of inequity

District and school leaders play an important role in introducing these types of guiding questions to prepare educators for coaching conversations applying the equity lens. Additionally, coaches can adapt and use these guiding questions in varied interactions to scaffold conversations aligned with the equity lens. To further operationalize how to use the equity lens in coaching and how coaching can work to reach equity-oriented outcomes, we unpack how to center equity in coaching. Specifically, the following section depicts equity audits, critical questioning, and observations of practice as three key equity-centered coaching routines.

GETTING CONCRETE ABOUT EQUITY-CENTERED COACHING

When achieving equity is a desired outcome of coaching, meaning that all students will be able to access and experience high-quality instruction that leads to higher achievement and better educational and life outcomes, it becomes vital to focus attention on the conditions that permit coaches to engage in equity-centered coaching. Leaders who engage coaches as part of an equity-focused improvement strategy attempt to build the capacity of the entire organization to tackle the beliefs, practices, and structures that exacerbate or reinforce inequities (Irby, 2021).

Coaches, serving in brave ways, can view equity issues and be the light that advances equity. More explicitly, coaches' work can account for (in)equities, staying focused on moving the needle to increase equity. In this book, we describe central coaching activities that center equity; these activities recognize that there are always places where the education system, schools, and educators leave students and communities behind. We encourage you to consider how to alter structures and practices to enable equity-centered coaching to construct more just schools.

Centering equity in coaching goes beyond reflecting on equity, calling out inequities, or examining biases. This means digging into the work and creating routines to make that happen (Roegman et al., 2019). Here, we delve into three high-leverage routines in equity-centered coaching. We show how, applying an equity lens, coaches can engage in equity audits, critical questioning, and observation of practice. The equity audit collects multiple measures of district and/or school data that not only represents a baseline for discovering existing disparities and disproportionalities, but monitors whether changes in dispositions, practices, policies, and structures are having the intended outcome (Roegman et al., 2019). Critical questioning involves coaches modeling a routine of critical reflection about the possibility of overt or implicit discrimination that leads to inequities in representation, access, participation, experiences, and/or outcomes.

Finally, observing practice with the application of the equity lens is a coaching routine that is not restricted solely to the classroom, nor to teachers alone. Instead, coaches should have opportunities to observe data team meetings, Professional Learning Community (PLC) routines, Planning and Placement Team processes for students who receive special education services, and leadership team meetings, since they are venues where practices, procedures, and policies are discussed and implemented with consequences for reinforcing or dismantling inequities. For coaching to matter, coaches should carry out these routines and experience an array of supports to sustain these efforts to counter racist and ableist structures, practices, and beliefs.

Equity Audit

In educational settings, equity audits are a routine for critically examining the policies, practices, programs, and structures that discriminate against students, families, or staff members as a result of their race, ethnicity, gender identity, sexual orientation, socioeconomic status, religion, country of origin, disability, age, or other factors that delineate social identity group membership. Coaches can facilitate an equity audit, including collecting baseline data to jump-start equity work. We have seen coaches center equity in the context of improvement efforts by collecting, analyzing, and disaggregating data in a manner that identifies disproportionalities and disparities that exist due to systemic inequities. Typically, educators launch these audits with quantitative data on student academic performance, participation, college and career readiness, and disciplinary outcomes. But, matching Safir and Dugan's (2021) suggestion, we encourage coaches to flip the data dashboard. This entails coaches starting with ground-level data incorporating voices, evidence, and artifacts of the student experience to view what is working within the system as well as point to systemic inequities throughout the system. In particular, this type of data plays a crucial role in uncovering stories of "hope and harm" (Safir & Dugan, 2021).

A quick online search for equity audits yields dozens of templates, frameworks, podcasts, and tools aiming to help educators gain insights regarding where there are disproportionalities in access and opportunity, and disparities in outcomes for various groups of students. However, for these tools, or equity audits, to be of their greatest use to districts and schools, they should be considered an organizational improvement routine that occurs at every level of the system on a regular basis. Therefore, equity audits should be collaborative, consistent, regularly repeated routines designed to build organizational capacity (Stevenson & Lemons, 2021). Here, we highlight how coaches should facilitate the equity audit routine by convening practitioners (e.g., instructional leadership teams, professional learning communities, and data teams) to analyze evidence and leverage their questioning and feedback techniques in the service of equity-oriented improvement. Simply stated, coaches should be seated at the table for equity audits, and coaching should entail the auditing of equity.

While conducting equity audits, which often surface disparities and disproportionalities, we caution against normalizing inequities such that leaders and practitioners shrug their shoulders and say, "Well, that's just how it is, these data tell the same story for these students everywhere, so why would it be different here." This quote unfortunately places the focus and blame on students, and it indicates educators are perpetuating stereotypes associated with intelligence, competence, and potential. Rather, equity audits should call out the systemic nature of gaps, interrogate their causation, and challenge practitioners to change structures and practices to promote more equitable outcomes. Coaches can play a major role in facilitating equity audits in their schools or districts, applying an equity lens to promote individual and organizational change which reduces inequities rather than merely measuring outcomes from a deficit stance.

Asking Critical Questions

Routinely asking critical questions within equity-centered coaching serves to unlock existing mental models about the existing district or school culture and create opportunities to challenge and change the status quo in teaching and leading. Within this, we borrow Sensoy and DiAngelo's (2017) description of critical thinking to put forth critical questioning as a strategy enabling coaches to work alongside coachees, "to think with complexity, to go below the surface when considering an issue and explore multiple dimensions and nuances" (p. 23). That is, by asking critical questions, coaches encourage a coachee to engage in thinking that accounts for multifaceted forms and outcomes of inequity. This routine of explicitly inquiring about equity issues has gained much popularity across the education field (Irby, 2021). Moreover, we have seen and supported a range of actors, from school board members and district administrators to coaches and teachers, in asking critical questions. Therefore, we delve into how coaches can ask critical questions as part of their work with a range of educators.

Questioning is a dominant feature in the landscape of coaching, and it does not stand alone—the greatest companion to questioning is listening. Skilled coaches are inquisitive, listening for what the coachee values and believes, and for how the coachee thinks and talks about problems of practice, as well as performance and learning goals. When engaging in critical questioning, coaches may ask questions to coachees and other educators about the following:

- The presence and impact of bias and stereotypes in policies, practices, and beliefs
- The diversity of representation—whose voice is being heard, and whose voice is absent
- The allocation of human, material, and financial resources based upon need rather than precedent

- The indicators for an equitable outcome—how will you know equity has been achieved based on the (intervention, treatment, strategy being deployed)
- Barriers inside and outside of the education system that create and perpetuate inequities

These questions create "friction" (Eberhardt, 2020), foreground equity issues, and allow educators to pause and consider new possibilities. Therefore, critical questions are at the heart of, in addition to serving as the trigger for, courageous conversations.

Importantly, these questions stretch from the individual and interpersonal levels to the organizational and system levels. We use the National Equity Project's *Levels of Systemic Oppression* to explain the varied ways in which biased interactions as well as policies ultimately impact the access, opportunities, experiences, and outcomes of students in our schools. Table 4.1 below provides examples of questions targeting reflection on inequitable structures and activities operating at varied levels.

Asking critical questions that center equity creates opportunities for self-reflection on behalf of the coachee and for crucial dialogue between practitioners. Questioning is a key lever for coaches, but it is not an

Table 4.1. Examples of critical questions targeting the individual, interpersonal, organizational, and system levels.

Level	Sample Question
Individual Level *Prejudice and biases held by the individual that impact beliefs about self and others*	Do I hold lower expectations for certain students in my classroom that prevent them from being able to access grade-level content?
Interpersonal Level *The ways that prejudice and biases manifest in relationships between people*	Am I regularly focusing my feedback to certain groups of students on their behaviors rather than their thinking?
Organizational Level *The ways that biases impact school practices and policies*	Does our schedule create the most disruptions for our most vulnerable students? Are we tracking students in a way that discriminates against race, social economic status, and language?
System Level *The ways that federal, state, and district policies reinforce discriminatory policies and practices across institutions*	Do district policies create barriers for access and opportunities for program participation that overwhelmingly disadvantage our students of color?

independent function. At their best, critical questions create openings that lead to opportunities for personal, institutional, and systemic examination and transformation. While they should not be solely responsible for asking questions that require a deep examination of self and system, coaches are skilled at questioning and, just as important, listening. Thus, they can serve as a model for what it sounds like to critically reflect upon inequities that plague school systems and, in response, portray possibilities to dismantle inequities.

As mentioned, coaches can ask questions that help leaders and teachers interrogate their assumptions, biases, and expectations. Moreover, through the critical questioning routine, coaches guide coachees in making new, different decisions about who receives opportunities and how to engage in new, different ways. When coaches support coachees in applying the equity lens to view varied aspects of teaching and leading, it can surface instances where individual beliefs have had a profound impact on interactions in the classroom, which in turn contribute to the normalized practices that have accumulated over time within the school and district. By conducting critical questioning, school and district leaders have a higher likelihood of rooting out practices and policies that exist by default and raise the risk of continuing to place students who have been historically marginalized at further disadvantage. When leaders continually examine equity gaps, encouraging coaches to engage in the core routine of critical questioning, they can reshape teaching, leading, and learning more equitably.

Equity-Focused Observations

We've named the equity audit and critical questioning as two key routines for coaches that serve to center equity by uncovering trends inside educational organizations as well as providing evidence on student experiences. We've also discussed coaches' use of an equity lens to support teachers and leaders to interrogate places throughout the system that disadvantage particular groups of students. Within equity-centered coaching, observations play a key role in detecting systemic issues and zooming into the experiences of particular groups of students, educators, families, and other people. Therefore, we explain how observations can function as a routine that intentionally and explicitly focuses on seeing inequity to boost the potential of coaching for reaching critical goals.

Coaching observations—whether they occur in classrooms or meetings, with groups or an individual—are venues where evidence is gathered to maintain a focus on equity. For example, when observing team meetings, coaches should listen for the language that staff and leaders use to describe student performance and behavior: Is deficit thinking driving the conversation, or are educators discussing the conditions that may be contributing to particular outcomes? And when observing instruction, coaches should look for evidence of how students are grouped and who is engaged in which activities; this can jump-start conversations with teachers about student grouping practices as well as how teachers make sense of student engagement.

Equity-centered coaching involves establishing routines for leaders, teachers, and teams to be observed in particular ways and for feedback to be given and received in particular ways to advance equity in the work of individuals as well as the whole organization. Coaches engaging in equity-focused observations should *not* operate as equity monitors or rely on an equity checklist. Rather, coaches should use their equity lens to closely focus on when, where, and how inequities surface in instruction and other schooling activities, and then to document evidence on this to share with others as a foundation for learning and change. We also invite coaches to collaboratively support teachers and leaders in engaging in experiences and conversations that challenge existing mental models about student capabilities and encourage a shift in practices to ensure historically marginalized students receive high-quality, equitable experiences and outcomes.

In addition to observing broad teaching moves or instructional routines linked with the district improvement strategy, coaches who center equity intentionally look for and take note of inequitable practices. This means that coaches focus on how they see and hear inequity during observations; coaches take snapshots of the equity landscape in their context. Next, coaches provide feedback, sharing evidence from those snapshots and naming equity issues, that assists the coachee in understanding their role in shifting practice to reduce inequities. For example, coaches can and should observe for issues including: which students are called upon to participate, and the length of time they are given to think before responding; how students are grouped; how unwanted behaviors are addressed, and to whom they are addressed; and how student feedback focuses on student thinking versus behavior and the degree to which feedback is constructive or critical; how leaders provide feedback to teachers of color; how leaders engage with BIPOC families.

CONNECTING STRATEGY TO EQUITY-CENTERED COACHING

Whether district and school leaders are embarking on equity-centered coaching or seeking to further target equity through coaching activities, it appears vital to examine how coaching is linked with the system's strategy. We encourage leaders to reflect and discuss the following questions: How is equity-centered coaching reflected in the strategic plan? How is it incorporated in the strategy map? How do planning documents and presentations mention equity-centered coaching? And how are leaders, teachers, and other constituents informed of the role of equity-centered coaching in efforts to enact the strategy? Analyzing the prioritization (or silence on) equity-centered coaching for equity as well as identifying the interconnections between equity and coaching provide crucial information on the nature of coaching. These steps are important so that leaders can refine both the strategy and the systems for equity-centered coaching in the context.

Bridging equity-centered coaching with strategy can reduce the inadvertent siloing of equity. We underscore that centering equity means that equity efforts should be everywhere in the organization and should be linked with all activities. To ensure equity permeates the organization, it is crucial for leaders to logically link equity-centered coaching to the broader strategy; this means weaving equity-centered coaching into multiple improvement efforts. For instance, equity-centered leadership coaching could address how principals can decrease gaps in college readiness for their Black and Latinx high school students. This could involve analyzing data across racial groups and practicing framing strategies to explicitly discuss gaps with teachers, other leaders, staff, and parents. And equity-centered literacy coaching could focus on how teachers can apply culturally sustaining practices while enacting writers' workshops. This could involve coaches modeling culturally sustaining writing instruction, including how to conference with students and encourage expression on students' intersecting identities.

Finally, to implement equity-centered coaching it is crucial to bring everyone on board, engaging multiple types of educators in the task of discussing and learning about inequities and then taking steps to work toward equity. This requires forming shared understandings of why the organization is moving in the direction of equity-oriented coaching and why this is a pivotal moment to engage in equity-oriented coaching. We assert it is not only targeted actors (e.g., district Equity Office administrators; school Equity Team members) who should be talking about equity; instead, all educators should be talking about and working toward equity. Indeed, distributing equity tasks among educators enables equity efforts to become both accepted and institutionalized across district and school levels. Finally, when diverse actors are implementing strategies and practices that work toward equity, this fosters collective learning for strategic, equitable improvement.

CONDITIONS ADVANCING EQUITY-CENTERED COACHING

Around 2010, equity coaching—as a brand of coaching on and for anti-racist leadership and teaching as well as culturally sustaining leadership and teaching (Aguilar, 2020)—burst onto the stage. In some cases, coaching models added attention to equity, while in other cases new coaching models emerged explicitly addressing equity in the face of mounting pressure to dismantle racist and ableist forces. Here, we depict equity-centered coaching, turning attention to particular affordances and limitations of structures and activities.

First, within the leadership coaching arena, equity coaches may engage with district and school leaders to reflect on background and privilege, practice strategies for engaging in anti-racist leadership, and address questions regarding challenges in advancing anti-racist practices in their context. Notably, these coaches are often positioned in intermediary organizations and, as such, they are external to the district or school. These coaches may facilitate professional learning activities with leaders and follow up with reflective work, yet there may be less time or protocols for side-by-side work in schools to improve equity-oriented leadership. In light of this, we encourage district leaders to consider how to extend, or embed, this form of equity coaching so that these leadership coaches can engage in activities alongside district and school leaders to see and hear the successes and challenges of carrying out anti-racist and culturally sustaining leadership. We assert this could assist in optimizing equity coaching by providing information to coaches to better structure their work with leaders.

Second, in the teacher coaching sphere, we have seen districts and schools employ equity coaches who concentrate on shifting teachers' practice to align to the tenets of culturally sustaining, inclusive instruction. In many cases, these coaches facilitate team and schoolwide PD on equity issues. This form of equity coaching, however, may inadvertently silo issues of social justice and equity. That is, these equity coaches may work in parallel with instructional or data coaches.

The preceding portrayal of the nascent state of equity-centered coaching shows variation in equity coaching as well as the way conditions remain shaky for this type of coaching. Rooted in our attention to the infrastructure that plays a role in optimizing coaching, we discuss five conditions with the potential to bolster equity-centered coaching, which includes:

- strategy;
- vision of quality, culturally responsive, teaching and leadership;
- resources;
- communication; and
- professional development.

First, the strategy—and each of its priorities—should be explicit about equity. Thus, if a district priority seeks to tackle racial inequity, then—instead of giving a generic nod to demographics or family background—the priority should point to the problem of racism or the necessity of countering racism in schools. Similarly, if a priority seeks to tackle inequities among students with disability, then it is important to point to the criticality of reducing ableism—rather than making hints about special needs or learning differences. Importantly, the district strategy must be concrete about equity so that coaches' strategic coaching can drive toward equity-oriented goals.

Second, weaving equity-centered coaching with strategy hinges on having a strong vision for and definition of high-quality instruction and leadership that specifically calls out culturally responsive teaching and leadership such that leaders are creating a school context that is responsive to the social, political, and environmental needs of marginalized students (Gay, 2018; Khalifa et al., 2016; Ladson-Billings, 1995). In other words, each district must flesh out what equitable teaching and leading look like, sound like, and feel like (Stevenson & Weiner, 2020).

We underscore that the vision is a system-level condition and, thus, district leaders hold key roles to develop and advance this vision. As we discuss in Chapter 5, a robust, strategic vision for high-quality instruction goes beyond standards and curriculum, since it depicts the big why and how to reach goals to benefit students. Similarly, a strong vision for quality leadership elevates and names core leadership moves with the potential to reduce inequities. As a step to align the vision with equity-oriented tenets, we encourage district leaders to analyze visions for and definitions of instruction and leadership to determine how they currently address equity and then revise statements and documents to clarify the link to equity. When carrying out these steps, leaders are *not* just drafting a plan or creating a color-coded diagram for their district website; rather, they are reflecting and learning together to strengthen and clarify the definition and operationalization of equity-centered coaching.

Third, the resources of time and space are vital so that leaders, teachers, and staff engage in meaningful collaboration regarding equity-centered coaching. Cutting to the chase, it takes time for educators to understand equity. Further, it takes time to develop shared understandings of the intersection of coaching and equity, gain techniques for detecting inequity during coaching, and formulate tactics to improve equity-oriented coaching. Because conversations on equity, identity, privilege, and bias entail asking critical questions, listening carefully, and following up in thoughtful, caring ways, we hearken these conversations are rarely brief or breezy (Singleton, 2014). However, these conversations must occur in—and for—equity-centered coaching.

Based upon this, carefully protected blocks of time for professional learning and coaching conversations are of the utmost importance. The time and space should be well designed so that trustful discussion unfolds in which educators ask hard questions about inequities, admit specific challenges in reaching equitable outcomes, assume there's room for improvement in the equity arena, and learn together to drive equitable change. Undeniably, consistent collaboration between coach and clients is necessary to institute and promote equity-centered coaching; this means carving out space for coaches to facilitate ongoing discussions on equity challenges as well as bright spots. Here, we wave the flag that leaders and coaches should not be running out of time on the agenda to answer questions about inequitable patterns in data or share reflections on anti-racist communication and leadership.

Fourth, consistent, clear communication about equity-centered coaching is necessary across levels of the system. Ongoing, transparent communication—about the interlinkage of equity, strategy, and coaching—signals that equity-centered coaching is a priority. More concretely, frequent communication reminds leaders and teachers that, yes, we, as coaches, have adopted equity-centered coaching, expecting it to occur across sites, and you will be experiencing equity-centered coaching. Simply stated: Equity-centered coaching is here (and will be sticking around!); it is important; and you will be engaging in this type of coaching. Additionally, regular, ongoing communication on equity-centered coaching helps set the norm that all discussions will include attention to inequity, such as asking questions about gaps for students of color and disabled students. Quite simply, a coach will *not* stop asking about equity, examining equity issues, and raising ideas on equity. And a coach will always engage in follow-up to see how practices are evolving, including whether and how changes are making a difference for marginalized groups of students.

A fifth condition enabling equity-centered coaching is professional development for coaches targeting strategic, equitable coaching; Chapter 6 offers additional details on coach PD. For coaches to have the knowledge and skills to conduct equity-centered coaching, they benefit from professional learning opportunities revolving around the tenets of equity-centered coaching, addressing the challenges of tackling racism and ableism in coaching, and given support on how they can attend to equity issues while carrying out multiple coaching practices (e.g., observing educators, providing feedback, analyzing data). We point to a coach professional learning community (PLC) as a structure enabling coaches to share challenges, spread ideas, and practice strategies to improve equity-centered coaching. In particular, a coach PLC has the potential to foster trust among coaches so that they confront inequities together. In particular, groups of coaches can learn about their own biases and gain strategies for dismantling deeply institutionalized, yet inequitable and deleterious, schooling practices. Within a coach PLC, coaches can grapple with how their biases and stereotypes disadvantage some students, while creating advantages for others. Further, they can reflect on how their biases about race, gender, ethnicity, and disability shape their engagement with students and adults in the district and school.

It takes time, energy, and support for coaches to engage in critical reflection, recognizing the role of personal and professional socialization, as well as the systemic nature of racism and other forms of oppression across our society. But this deep and critical self-reflection provides coaches with a stronger ability to identify the most common places within the teacher practice where discretion can lead to discrimination. As a result, these coaches can recognize the defensive routines that permeate collaborative conversations about schooling, instruction, academic performance, and student behavior, and how that defensiveness shuts down opportunities to interrogate individual and collective bias. And these coaches can see where and how district and school policies create barriers for specific student groups who are consistently undervalued and underserved. Finally, coaches who engage in this level of self-reflection are instilled with the habit of asking, and continually checking: Who is being left behind? Who is being underserved? How can we work to better serve those students, those families, and those communities? Acknowledging resources and supports are necessary to enable equity-centered coaching to unfold in districts and schools, we presented key conditions promoting equity-centered coaching. Next, we describe how reformers and leaders can design systems and refine coaching systems that explicitly center equity and provide a foundation for equity-centered coaching.

DESIGNING COACHING SYSTEMS THAT CENTER EQUITY

To make equity-centered coaching matter, in which coaches center equity and educational organizations take strides toward equity, the complete system and its leaders must center equity. This may mean changing the goals, priorities, and resources of an organization. Moreover, coaching models must intentionally center equity. Regardless of their structure (e.g., district or school based), format, activities, or foci (e.g., leadership, data, science, elementary ELA), they are advancing individual and organizational learning to reach equitable outcomes. Thus, coaching routines, including observation–feedback cycles and leader-support conversations, should be linked to challenges of inequity and grapple with how the coachee can shift their work to help resolve inequities in their context. For example, a math coach's observations could target how the teachers uses inclusive approaches to meet the needs of students with disabilities. And, as another example, leadership coaching could include feedback on how the principal communicates with families in culturally sustaining ways.

As district leaders design and refine coaching models squarely centered on equity, it is important for them to look upwards and outwards to structures enabling (or impeding) coaches to carry out equity-oriented work. That is, what is the nature of the procedures and protocols for hiring, supervising, and supporting coaches? And how do these proto-cols and procedures ensure that coaches are, at the outset, selected and developed so that they are well prepared to engage in strategic, equity-oriented coaching? We propose that, at the hiring phase, the coach job description as well as the coach selection process should explicitly attend to equity-centered coaching. We encourage system leaders to enumerate, in job descriptions, that coaches will be expected to engage with others around equity challenges and work toward equity-oriented goals. In this way, leaders will be concrete about the way equity and strategy fit with coaches' work. Additionally, we encourage leaders to ask coach applicants to articulate their orientation toward equity, explain how they've engaged in equity-centered work, and also share how they view the link between coaching and equity. Leaders can use these responses as evidence of aspiring coaches' strengths and areas of opportunity.

With awareness that selecting and hiring equity-centered coaches are merely initial steps for promoting equity-centered coaching, we also attend to the ways the supervision and development of coaches could place weight on equity-centered coaching. This could involve PD on the tenets and practices of equity-centered coaching, including how to conduct equity audits and how to facilitate courageous conversations with teachers, principals, and other actors on what they've observed, and what evidence they've gathered (Singleton, 2014). Perhaps even more importantly, system and school leaders should coach coaches on how and why to center equity. This symmetry could involve leaders modeling and explicitly explaining their equity-centered work to coaches. It could also involve providing coaches with feedback on their equity-centered coaching tasks, including strengths and areas of improvement in their auditing work, critical questioning, and classroom or leadership observations. Providing ongoing, tailored support regarding grappling with equity issues is crucial so that coaches develop understandings of how to engage in—and persist with—this type of coaching.

Finally, to make coaching matter, system leaders should engage in continuous improvement techniques to determine how coaches are centering equity and how to improve conditions so that coaches can center equity throughout their work. In Chapter 5, we go into greater depth on the continuous improvement of strategic, equity-centered coaching. This involves collecting and analyzing multiple forms of evidence on coaching to view strengths and areas of opportunity and then designing solutions, or refining approaches, to match local needs. And these improvement cycles should always revolve around the question: How is coaching functioning to reduce inequity? We underscore that, by conducting such improvement cycles, leaders pull back the curtain on efforts to continually refine coaching as an instrument to reach significant equity-oriented goals. In so doing, they reveal the necessity of learning and striving, rather than remaining stagnant, to improve teaching, leading, and students' experiences and outcomes.

TO MAKE COACHING MATTER

This chapter illuminated principles and practices of equity-centered coaching; next, we offer concrete suggestions for how district leaders, principals, and coaches can assemble positive conditions for—and implement—equity-centered coaching. Each of these actors hold unique responsibilities for equity-centered coaching, yet their collaboration matters, including explicitly communicating about inequities and equity-oriented goals and learning together about how to promote and support equity-centered coaching and, ultimately, move their system toward crucial goals.

District leaders should:

- be explicit about equity in their strategic plan;
- provide robust explanations for why and how coaches will engage in equity-centered activities; and
- hire, develop, and support coaches to conduct equity-centered routines and work toward reaching equitable outcomes.

Principals should:

- provide conditions for coaches to conduct equity-centered routines;
- collaborate with coaches around equity challenges and opportunities;
- share multiple forms of evidence tied to equity issues with coaches; and
- provide ongoing, professional learning experiences that address the context for why equity matters and explain tenets of equity-centered coaching.

Coaches should:

- elevate equity in all improvement efforts and reforms, either at the district or school level;
- devote time for critical questioning, observations, and equity audits to further equity-oriented goals; and
- participate in ongoing professional development to gain capacity in facilitating conversations about race, bias, and oppression.

For coaching to matter, the policies, structures, models, routines, practices, norms, and conceptualizations of coaching must center equity. This chapter presented how equity-centered coaching confronts persistent inequities across educational organizations, leading, and teaching. It shared how coaches' work routines can deploy the equity lens. Chapter 4 also articulated the urgency of refining coaching models and professional supports for coaches to assist in reaching equity-oriented goals. In this manner, we emphasized the importance of the infrastructure for coaching. Chapter 5, too, interrogates the infrastructure for coaching by presenting the relationship between coaching and strategy. Specifically, Chapter 5 discusses how coaching functions as an instrument to advance district improvement strategy, how coaches' work aligns to strategy, and how strategic plans enable equity-centered coaching. We highlight, therefore, how a coherent, systemic approach to coaching aids so that it reaches its full potential within districts and schools.

Connecting Strategy and Coaching

Hope is not a strategy.

—Vince Lombardi

Reformers and leaders have high hopes for coaching. But coaching is not a magic wand; it does not automatically improve individual nor organizational outcomes. Rather, system and school leaders must intentionally—and explicitly—link coaching and the district improvement strategy. This chapter explores how coaching supports improvement as part of strategy. We discuss elements of a powerful strategy, how coaching ought to be designed to support that strategy, and the work of leaders to ensure that occurs. We are acutely aware that both districtwide strategy and coaching models are not easy to create or sustain and that very few districts have successfully connected coaching with strategy. This chapter aims to provide leaders with ways of thinking about coaching and strategy that improve them both and increase the coordination between them.

When we get a call about working with a district on coaching, the conversation frequently sounds like this:

> *District Math Coordinator:* We have had math specialists in the district for seven or eight years now. We hired them when we were looking to implement a new math program. Then when we selected our new math program, their job was to roll out the curriculum through 6th grade. Then, we started looking at math in middle and high school. Now we are interested in moving them more toward being coaches, and we'd like to talk to you about supporting that shift.
>
> *Us:* Great. What do you think that might look like?
>
> *District Math Coordinator:* Well, obviously we'd like to have coaching cycles, so we were hoping to have you train the coaches (formerly the math specialists), and then we have questions about how many teachers the coaches can coach, what coaching cycles look like, and so on. Because, you know, frequently when they observe a teacher, they come back and say, they're not

getting the most out of the math program because they don't have great classroom management, or they spend too much time talking to the kids and the kids never get to practice problem solving for themselves. And I also think we need to work on creating the conditions for coaching by working with the building leaders.

Us: Great. So, you've already done work on creating a Portrait of a Graduate? Do you think everyone knows what that is?

District Math Coordinator: Yes, we call it our Vision of a Learner. And yes, we surveyed teachers, parents, and students last year as part of our strategic planning process, and that showed us that everyone knows about the Vision of a Learner. I mean, not everyone was perfectly clear about what it says or how it influences what we teach, but we were pretty happy about how familiar people were with it.

Us: Great. And what about a shared understanding of what high-quality instruction looks like, do you have that?

District Math Coordinator: Hmmm, let me think about that. . . . Well, that's not something that we've ever really talked about at a district level. I mean, obviously, we're very invested in all students experiencing effective instruction, but that's the purview of individual principals, to lead for that, in their schools.

Us: Great. So, when it comes to the coaches, there isn't a clear picture of what they are coaching toward? Each coach is doing what he or she thinks is best?

District Math Coordinator: I believe that is accurate, yes.

Us: So, is that something that you might work on, as part of developing a coaching model?

District Math Coordinator: Well, I would have to get the assistant superintendent to make that a priority, and I'm not sure she really sees that as an added value. So right now, I'm more focused on building the skills of the coaches and getting the building administrators to buy into the idea of more coaching.

This conversation, taken from our notes of an initial conversation with a district math coordinator, illustrates a quandary of coaching. The vague concept that senior district leaders have of coaching is that it is a strategy for improving educational outcomes. But in practice, coaching is enacted as an individual- or organizational-level professional learning activity, and the potential of coaching to have an impact on the system as a whole is unfulfilled, or at least impeded. Often, this happens even when the leaders who have the power to create the enabling conditions for coaching to operate at the system level, such as the assistant superintendent in our example, believe that they are, in fact, implementing coaching as a systemic intervention. How is this possible? Partly because leaders don't always have a good grasp of what coaching is and how it can be optimized, and partly because they don't always have good methods for conceptualizing and creating strategy. Thus, in the following section, we lay an overview of implementing strategic plans to achieve equitable goals at the district level.

OVERVIEW OF STRATEGIC PLANS AND STRATEGY

Boards of education often adopt formal policies or informal practices that require the creation of a district strategic plan, frequently on a five-year cycle. The development process is composed of a set of activities: typically beginning with a visioning process, stakeholder involvement, setting goals, and drafting priorities, and then followed by the creation of action plans that include benchmarks and outcome measures. This process is frequently large and unwieldy, and completing it becomes an end in itself, leading to a plan that has more to do with fulfilling board requirements than with improving outcomes for students. The process may yield multicolored diagrams and a flashy website. Optimizing coaching requires getting rid of the trappings of strategic planning and replacing it with thinking about strategy in a way that is both simpler and deeper.

Strategic thinking entails the ability to establish an objective (also known as a vision); rally others around the vision (also known as inspiration or motivation); weigh options; devise a ploy or stratagem to reach the vision; break the vision down into smaller, proximate goals; devise plans to enact the strategy (by focusing, for example, on the attainment of proximate goals); manage competing expectations and constituencies; compromise; and base all intermediate decisions on their role in reaching the ultimate objective (deferral of gratification is an illustration of strategic thinking). School and district leaders immediately recognize these skills as what they do on an hourly basis, but rarely possess a mechanism for connecting the strategic thinking they do with the strategic plan they have designed.

The existence of a district strategic plan is ubiquitous and often taken for granted. But the existence of a strategic plan does not guarantee ties to either strategic thinking or continuous improvement. In particular, strategic planning is frequently divorced from leaders' strategic thinking. This chapter grapples with the following interrelated questions: How should educational leaders think about strategy while enacting a coaching program? How does coaching fit with a school or district's strategy for improving student learning? How can the design, implementation, and monitoring of strategy be improved by and through coaching? And what supports need to be in place so that coaching can assist with reaching strategic goals? By tackling these questions, we make the case that coaching should be a catalyst for making progress toward the vision of the district, as opposed to simply a professional learning mechanism. Coaching can be a powerful lever for both improving the practice of teachers and leaders individually, as well as supporting organizational change in the service of the district's vision. Further, these two activities are not separate from each other. The ability of coaching to improve teaching and leading is moderated by the strength of the organizational support for coaching and district coherence around high-quality instruction.

THE MEANING, HISTORY, AND IMPORTANCE OF STRATEGY

In education, the words strategy, strategies, and strategic are used in different contexts to mean different things. For example, many use the term instructional strategies to denote the range of techniques, routines, and practices that teachers use to engage students with content. In the realm of educational leadership, strategy is strongly linked to strategic planning, and more specifically to the strategic plan, which is part of typical district operations. We define strategy as "an informed and intentional set of aligned choices about actions to generate a desired outcome," built on four principles: equity, logic, capacity, and coherence (Stevenson & Weiner, 2020). In practice, this means that the strategy should have equity at its core, because in education, the desired outcome is, ultimately, about improving outcomes for all students while ensuring students' opportunities and experiences are optimized. Absolutely *everything* that educational leaders prioritize, plan, implement, and fund must be in service of equity.

Ensuring that strategy is logical involves designing strategy by backwards mapping from the desired outcome, so that the throughline from the work of the superintendent to the classroom experience of students is clear. There should be an articulated chain of causation from district priorities and district leaders' work to teaching and learning. Designing a strategy must also include building capacity since making change in schools necessitates multiple actors learning multiple things. Finally, the strategy should be coherent, so there is a shared understanding of what the strategy is, what it is designed to achieve, how parts fit together, and what it means to be executing it well. This ensures all oars are rowing in the same direction.

Strategy became a feature of commercial thinking with the rise of the large corporation and the subsequent emergence of business as a subject of academic study, with publications on the role of strategy in successful corporations starting to appear in the 1950s. The proliferation of books on strategy fueled interest in the subject, and companies began creating specialist roles to work on the various aspects of corporate strategy, including far-reaching data collection and elaborate strategic planning processes.

The intricate plans that were written assumed, however, that the world is a rational and orderly place, and that the challenges that the plans were designed to overcome were technical in nature. In other words, that the problems plus solutions were known, and so all that organizations had to do was to plan and execute the strategy to produce success. But not all challenges are technical, not all problems are knowable in advance, and not all solutions have already been invented so that they may be deployed when the need arises.

Across the business sector, the linearity of "old style" strategic planning has mainly been overtaken by the notion of conducting cycles of continuous improvement (Edmondson & Verdin, 2017). A hallmark of continuous improvement is understanding and testing to improve (Deming, 1982). Continuous improvement also uses data, but the work of using data to improve processes to improve outcomes is intentionally conducted by the actors most directly involved in creating those outcomes.

In education, however, strategic planning and continuous improvement frequently exist side by side without intentional or productive connections between them, and educational leaders commonly bemoan the lack of connection between the two processes. Most districts have a strategic plan created through a process of stakeholder involvement and adopted by the board of education, and also a mechanism for involving teachers to continuously improve their practice (e.g., the PLC model described by DuFour and Eaker [1998] or Data Wise as discussed by Boudett and colleagues [2020]). Educational leaders see how the strategic plan rarely drives the daily work of schools and teachers, and they also recognize how data teams and PLCs lack direction and, as a result, fail to have an impact on classroom instruction or student outcomes.

A core pillar of our argument is that coaching, for it to be worth the investment and for it to advance improvement, must be strategic. Here, we are not referring to coaches' work, although that, too, should be strategic. We are referring to the importance of strong, logical relationships between coaching as a program, strategic priorities, and improved outcomes for students. Our experience working in the field, as well as our analysis of district plans, leads us to the conclusion that coaching is not reliably strategic. In other words, it is frequently unclear—to the coaches, their clients, and other constituents—what the relationship is between coaching and the larger vision of the district, what the role of coaches is in enacting the district strategy, how coaching will be monitored and improved, and what supports will be put in place to maximize its chances of success. Consequently, coaching may function to improve something that isn't a priority, or it may not be properly supported so that coaches can concentrate priorities. Next, we suggest how leaders can address some of these issues by treating coaching as a component of the improvement strategy of the system.

THE RELATIONSHIP BETWEEN COACHING AND STRATEGY

For coaching to increase the odds that a strategy will succeed, the strategy itself needs to be logical and powerful, and it needs to clearly show how coaching fits into it. We underscore that coaching should be seen not as *a* strategy but as part of *the* strategy. That is, policymakers, leaders, and educators should treat coaching as a vehicle that drives the improvement strategy forward. This means positioning coaches as leaders who amplify strategy.

Coaching is one of the informed and intentional choices a district makes to generate a desired outcome; it is a component of the strategy. Coaching exists not as an end in itself but in service of a larger vision. Figure 5.1 shows the relationship between a coaching model and a district's strategy for improvement. A coherent coaching model is a desirable step, yet this must be coupled with a high-potential strategy, so that they reinforce each other. A coherent coaching model woven with a strong strategy aligns change efforts and raises the likelihood of improving students' educational experiences and outcomes.

We propose that the starting point for educational leaders aiming to connect coaching to a broader strategy is to answer the following questions. Their responses to these questions assist in identifying resources to design, implement, and refine the coaching system in a manner that

Figure 5.1. A model showing how the improvement strategy and coaching model are mutually reinforcing.

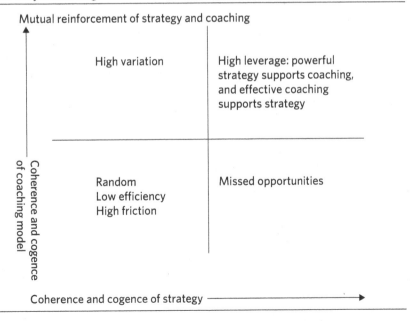

coherently works toward improvements in student leading, teaching, and student outcomes.

1. What goals do we have for students, when they leave us at graduation and every year before then?
2. What do the curriculum and instruction need to look like in order for us to meet our goals for students?
3. What capacity do we need to build in teachers so that they can provide the intended curriculum and instruction for students?
4. How is coaching going to support teachers in teaching the curriculum and instruction we expect?
5. What capacity do we need to build in coaches so that they can support teachers the way we need them to?
6. How are building and district leaders going to support coaches' development?
7. What other systems, structures, and resources need to be in place?

Note that these questions don't start with coaching. Instead, they start with the intended outcomes that a district aspires to and that the district's strategy intends to lead toward. This approach to strategy development is an exercise in backwards mapping (Stevenson & Weiner, 2020). More explicitly, strategy development involves creating a map with the inputs, levers, and outcomes tied to the strategy to reach strategic goals. A strategy map for coaching shows not only how coaches are expected to coach teachers, but also how teachers are expected to teach students. Therefore, the strategy map acts as an anchor for the development of a shared understanding of what high-quality coaching and teaching look like. Further, this map describes the work that leaders must do to support the development of coaches and the broader implementation of coaching across the system.

It is crucial to add that the development of a shared understanding of what good coaching and teaching look like has the benefit of taking the coach out of the role of arbiter of quality. The absence of a shared mental model of good teaching puts the coach in the position of being the teacher of the teacher, rather than the coach, to illustrate what "good teaching" looks like. We frequently hear school and district leaders bemoan the fact that teachers are not self-reflective, or don't self-assess. Yet, we know that everyone is capable of self-assessment if they have a clear sense about the target for high-quality performance that they are being assessed against.

Many districts assume that, because they have a teacher evaluation rubric, that the target, or nature of quality instruction, is clear, but that is not always the case. A shared mental model of quality teaching is not something that can solely be written and then transmitted to someone else; it emerges from engagement over time. Coaches can support teachers in reflecting on how they're enacting the district's vision of quality teaching. All this is not to say that coaching construed simply as a relationship between coach and client will not be useful. Coaching relationship has the potential to be valuable to the client and rewarding for the coach, and many coaching relationships don't have a purpose beyond the benefit of the client. But, for coaching to fully pay off as a mechanism for systemic improvement, it needs to be tied to strategy.

We have seen districts employ coaching in a variety of ways, some more effectively than others, and with some creating tighter couplings between their coaching model and district strategy. The following examples illustrate various states of strategy that contribute to an array of opportunities and challenges for the implementation of coaching. Across these examples, we encourage examining how and why leaders did or did not couple the coaching model to district improvement strategy. In District A, coaching was adopted as a response to low literacy scores, without much thought given to building a coherent coaching model or a district strategy—the lower left quadrant of Figure 5.1. In District B, there is both a coherent coaching model and a well-constructed district strategy—the sweet spot represented by the top right quadrant of Figure 5.1. District C, on the other hand, does not fit neatly on the quadrants; the issue in this district is not so much the strength of the strategy or the coaching model, but how well coaching is executed and supported by the district leadership.

District A: Coaching as a Random Act of Improvement

In District A, the superintendent was under considerable pressure from the school board to improve student standardized test scores in reading, as they were noticeably lower than in neighboring districts. In fact, the board practically insisted that the superintendent hire coaches for teachers in grades K through 4 as the solution to raising test scores. So, within a few weeks, the district advertised for and hired a literacy coach for every elementary school in the district, with a mandate to improve test scores. The job description required that applicants show that they were exemplary teachers, and had some leadership experience, such as being a grade-level team leader. The job description did not require previous experience as a coach, and the district provided coaching training through a well-known coaching organization to the newly hired coaches.

When we became involved with the district several years later to help with strategic planning, we asked about the role of the coaches in supporting the strategy, since changing instructional practices was a major element of the strategy. The superintendent became a bit agitated. She expressed frustration that the district had had coaches for six years but literacy scores still had not improved. She talked about the millions of dollars that the district had spent on salaries for coaches—with no return on investment. When we suggested that they might have an important part to play in supporting teachers under the new instructional model, she was unconvinced. She had lost faith in the potential of coaching to move the needle.

We don't mean to make it sound as though the adoption of coaching in District A was without purpose. But coaching rested on a weak theory of action; the supposition was that *if* the district hired successful reading teachers, trained them to be coaches, and deployed them to coach less experienced teachers, *then* the less experienced teachers would improve their practice, and reading achievement would improve. This theory turned out to have several gaps, including:

- The teachers were not clear why they were being assigned a coach, and so some worried that they were in trouble or at risk. They feared negative judgment, so they never really let their guard down to the coaches; they didn't talk about their struggles or allow themselves to be observed trying new/difficult techniques.
- In turn, the coaches saw teachers as defensive and resistant and spent their time only with teachers who wanted to be coached, and there weren't many of them. The coaches' perceived self-efficacy was damaged—they didn't see themselves as having the potential to make a difference for students or their school.
- The coaches were not clear on what exactly they were expected to do. In the absence of clear direction from the district as to what they were coaching toward, the coaches relied on their own understanding of best practices and were easily swayed or deployed to take on supplemental activities, which exacerbated variation among teachers' practices.
- The principals were not clear how the coaches fit into their school improvement plans. In consequence, they neglected to include them in essential decisions and actions pertaining to instructional improvement, such as the topics for, and delivery of, professional development of teachers. Principals rarely distributed leadership to coaches in a substantive way. They also pulled them from coaching for needs that they saw as more important, such as lunch duty and substitute teaching.

Coaching in District A was not attached to a district strategy, because there was no strategy. The superintendent had neither fully charted the connection between coaching and improved outcomes, nor had she anticipated the support and infrastructure that coaching requires.

District B: Coaching as Part of a Well-Designed Strategy

In District B, we saw a very different, and more tightly coupled, approach. The superintendent of this district realized that, although the standardized test scores looked all right when compared to neighboring districts, a deeper look revealed that measures of student achievement indicated that year-to-year student growth was not as great as expected. Based on this, she and her leadership team did some investigating, including talking to teachers, and came to some conclusions about the lack of a focused approach to reading instruction across the district. In particular, the previous literacy director had "never met a program he didn't like," and while the new literacy director had created a much more streamlined literacy program, teachers were not always clear on what they should be doing. As part of an effort to foster coherent, high-quality literacy instruction to promote student growth, the superintendent, in conjunction with a task force that included central office, principals, and teachers, developed a strategy that answered the questions from earlier in this chapter:

1. What goals do we have for students in literacy when they go to middle school, and every year before then?
2. What do the curriculum and instruction we provide need to look like in order for students to meet those goals?
3. What capacity do we need to build in teachers so that they can provide the intended curriculum and instruction in reading for students?
4. How are building and district leaders going to support coaches' development (time, resources, culture, etc.)?
5. What other systems, structures, and resources need to be in place?

The answers to these questions became the new District B Literacy Model. Since this district did not yet have coaches, the plan did not include a coaching model or any reference to coaches. But as the planning process continued, it became clear that the building leaders did not believe that they had the time, knowledge, or skill to provide the level of support needed for teachers to successfully adopt the new literacy model. District leaders came to realize that building the capacity of teachers would require a level of technical expertise and ongoing support that principals were not able to provide.

At this point, the superintendent asked the literacy director to put together a plan for coaching in the district that would include a coaching model specific to supporting the district's literacy program and a plan for identifying, recruiting, and supporting coaches best suited for the literacy program and the coaching model. Specifically, the superintendent wanted to know whether it would make more sense to hire experienced coaches, perhaps from outside the district, or to adopt a "grow-your-own" approach since it would be more effective and/or cost effective to hire coaches already familiar with the district. Since the district had developed a literacy model that was explicit about the literacy instruction that was to be provided to students, creating a job description and hiring criteria for the new coaches was a relatively straightforward task, and actually acted as a check to see whether the language in the literacy model was sufficiently clear and detailed.

The theory of action in District B, therefore, is much stronger than in District A: *If* there is a clear and shared understanding of the vision we have for the success of all our students, and *if* the district adopts a curriculum aligned to that vision; and *if* the district develops a shared understanding of high-quality instruction; and *if* teachers receive support to enact the instructional program that includes coaching; *then* students are more likely to acquire the knowledge, skills, and dispositions described in the vision.

District B's theory of action has a clear logic to it, and, when fleshed out, it will become a strategy. Answers to these questions, for example, might help district leaders to revise the improvement strategy: How will principals know how to create the conditions for coaching to be successful in their schools? Who is responsible for communicating to teachers that coaching is a district priority to support implementation of the strategy, rather than to shore up weak teachers? How will fiscally sensitive board members be sold on the need to invest in coaching? Once these questions are answered, district leaders would be on their way to connecting coaching to the district strategy in a more aligned, powerful manner.

District C: Coaching as an Undersupported District Program

Such a stark illustration of coaching unmoored from a cogent vision for improvement as described from District A is uncommon. But, so is District B's well-designed and well-executed plan. Much more common is something in between, which we portray as follows.

In District C, there is, indeed, a coaching model, which was developed several years ago when coaching was first adopted in the district. At that time, a lot of effort was put into "launching" coaching: Coaches were hired and trained, there was a clever visual of the coaching model, and the superintendent proudly discussed the coaching initiative with school board members and other constituents. However, there are multiple signals that coaching is not functioning as a high-leverage driver of improvement. We briefly describe these signals and encourage identifying how leaders can strengthen the coaching system to more effectively function as part of the current district-improvement strategy.

- The coaching model was developed by a small team, at the behest of the superintendent. The plan for coaching was distributed to principals, but was not widely discussed with teachers. Thus, coaching is seen as something that is done to, rather than with, teachers.

- Teachers' understanding of how coaching is supposed to work is vague, and so they are not well equipped to engage in coaching. They worry that being coached is an indicator that their principal or department head thinks that they are unsatisfactory instructors.
- Similarly, principals hold vague understandings of coaching, including how coaches' work links to instructional leadership, strategy, and equity. Principals are also not clear on the role of the coaches, so in some buildings they coach and have no additional duties. Yet in other buildings, coaches are the pinch-hitters when the building is short of substitute teachers or someone to supervise lunch or recess, and within other schools, coaches spend the majority of their time working directly with students as interventionists.
- A lot of turnover has taken place since the initial introduction of coaching in the district, and the educators who recently joined the district never received a coaching orientation. In other words, leaders assume an institutionalization of coaching that never fully occurred.

Thus, in District C, coaching looks as though it is connected to the larger work of the district, but in fact it is unmoored and ineffective. The work of putting together a coaching model, as well as the investments in employing and training coaches, may not be wasted, but those efforts certainly have not generated the desired dividends. To realize the potential of coaching, system and school leaders need to clarify, support, and integrate coaching into the mission and work of the organization.

THE WORK OF LEADERS TO SUPPORT STRATEGIC COACHING

Designing a strategy that includes coaching as an instrument is an important task, but the work does not stop there. For coaching to be deployed successfully in service of the district vision and to reach challenging goals, structures must be put in place enabling coaches to do their best work, and enabling coaching to occur in schools, meeting rooms, and classrooms. In the remainder of this chapter, we describe the conditions that district and school leaders should put in place to increase the likelihood of coaching to fulfill its potential to drive forward the district's improvement strategy.

Create a Coaching Model Aligned With the Strategy

As we will discuss in Chapter 8, many versions of coaching are adopted across the education field. And while these models share many commonalities, they are also different enough that the coaching should be tailored to the goals and the circumstances. For example, if coaching is intended to support new teachers in improving their technical skills at teaching reading or behavior management, then bug-in-ear coaching may be effective even though experienced educators may find the idea intrusive (or even appalling). But if coaching is intended to support experienced teachers in designing formative assessments, a peer-coaching model may be fruitful.

It is not always obvious whether a coaching model will work in a context or match the strategy. The models promoted by myriad texts on coaching do not always make it straightforward for potential adopters to ascertain whether a specific model is a good match for their situation. A coaching model needs to be a match along two dimensions: the learning stage of the client and the kind of skill needed for successful performance. On the first dimension, the more novice the client, the more they need feedback on the task. The more experienced they are, the more they benefit from coaching that supports them in self-regulation (Hattie & Clarke, 2018). On the second dimension, the type of work typically performed by the client may be more technical in nature, meaning that there is a known effective way to do the work; or the client's work may be more adaptive, meaning that the problems are multifaceted and the solutions are context-dependent (Heifetz & Laurie, 1997). If the work is technical, then task-level feedback is more often appropriate. In contrast, if the work is more adaptive, process-level or self-regulation feedback becomes much more appropriate.

In a *New Yorker* article, Atul Gawande (2011) describes how he benefited from coaching. Gawande is an experienced surgeon, and he asked a fellow surgeon to observe him operate and give him feedback afterwards. The types of surgery he performs require a great deal of technical skill, and so his coach gives him task-related feedback. This provides a great example of a certain type of coaching. A superintendent, however, is a very different kind of professional; much of the work they perform requires knowledge and experience, but, because they rarely face the same challenge twice, and they work in a unique district context, the nature of the work is much more adaptive. A superintendent coach, therefore, will rarely give technical advice because the right answer is not known; instead, the coach will support the superintendent's thinking as they weigh their options and decide how to approach contextualized problems. It is not that the superintendent's work is more difficult than the surgeon's or that they are less experienced; rather, the nature of the work varies.

Create Coherence Around Coaching

Our author team has engaged with districts on a variety of improvement projects, including strategic planning and leadership development. As part of this, we gather information about teachers' and leaders' perceptions of the district's goals, their strategic priorities, and how those priorities will help the district reach its goals. During these efforts, it is often the case that educators cannot say what the district is working on, either because of lack of communication from the senior leadership or because the district is working on so many things simultaneously that it is difficult to say what the focus is. The lack of understanding of how teachers' and leaders' work are interconnected and interdependent contributes to several challenges. Educators are hindered from supporting each other without shared mental models of the strategy or without knowing how to execute it. It is unclear where attention, effort, and resources should be directed to create the most improvement.

Coherence, on the other hand, is a shared understanding of performance, and the processes for generating quality performance. And coherence leads to improvements in performance and processes (Kozlowski & Ilgen, 2006). There are great benefits in creating coherence among team or organization members when they share responsibility for the generation of an outcome. Where coaching is concerned, coherence is complicated. Not only must educators have a shared mental model of what good teaching and leading look like and how they work together, but they also need to have a shared understanding with another group of educators, the coaches, regarding what good coaching looks like and how they should work with the coaches. Moreover, the coaches themselves need to have a shared understanding of what good teaching and leading look like, what good coaching looks like, and how they should be working with teachers and leaders. These interlocking mental models require time and extended dialogue to create and maintain.

In our work with districts, we frequently encounter frustration among coaches regarding the lack of a coaching model. And—even if a coaching model exists—it is frequently opaque to the leaders who are supposed to support it. And there is almost never any attention paid to the understanding that teachers have of coaching, beyond any expectations that are placed on them regarding their participation in coaching. These are signals of incoherence regarding what coaching is, and how and why to engage in coaching. But these are also indicators of a larger issue in the district, including lack of shared understanding of the vision and strategy of the district, and/or the connection of coaching to that strategy, and/or a lack of clarity as to how the district defines quality teaching.

Coaching is a significant investment in improving the performance of teachers and leaders. Given what we know about the power of shared understandings of reform (Spillane et al., 2002), it is highly logical that an organization investing in coaching should also invest in creating coherence across all levels regarding what quality coaching looks like and how it is supposed to improve the performance of those being coached. Within this, coachees, as well as the coaches themselves, should be involved in conversations to formulate shared understandings regarding coaching. Effective coaching requires not only the creation of that shared understanding, but also leaders who will work to create clear, consistent framings of coaching (Mangin & Dunsmore, 2015; Woulfin, 2020).

Providing Enabling and Transparent Logistics

Quite often when we do see coaching mentioned in district strategic plans or school improvement plans, only the technical details of the coaching plan (such as how many coaches will be hired or who will supervise them) are included (Stevenson, 2017). However, the planning concerning coaching should not be limited to logistics such as setting up regular coaching meetings or coaches turning in coaching logs. Table 5.1 lists responsibilities for the logistical aspects of making coaching work across levels of the education system. Within this, we highlight that defining the nature of coaching—and offering supports for coaching—boosts clarity for administrators, coachees, and coaches.

Table 5.1. Key logistical tasks of district and school administrators and coaches and coachees for implementing coaching.

Type of Educator	Tasks
District administrators	• Securing the budget for coaching • Orchestrating the creation of a district coaching model • Aligning coaching with the district strategy for improvement • Hiring and training coaches (see Chapter 6 on building capacity for coaching) • Communicating to building leaders and teachers the expectations around coaching • Routines to collect and analyze evidence on the nature and effectiveness of coaching (see Chapter 7 on continually improving coaching)
School administrators	• Setting schedules permitting coach–teacher collaboration • Collaborating with the coach • Supporting and developing coaches (see Chapter 6 on building capacity for coaching) • Developing coaches' understanding of the school's strategic goals and priorities • Communicating to teachers the purposes of and expectations for coaching
Coach	• Communicating to building leaders about strengths and gaps in conditions for coaching • Communicating to teachers the purposes of and expectations for coaching • Developing clients' understanding of how to engage in different forms of coaching • Enacting coaching routines in a consistent manner • Collaborating with district and school leaders to promote coherence
Coachee	• Engaging in coaching routines in a consistent manner • Responding to coach communication • Communicating to building leaders and coaches about strengths and gaps in the coaching system

The logistics, or technical details, of the coaching model are quite important to multiple actors for multiple reasons. That is, these logistics matter to coaches, whose working lives are directly affected by the nature of the model, but they also matter to coachees, who want to know when, where, and how to engage in coaching. Additionally, since administrators must create conditions for coaching, they also need to fully understand the logistics of the model. In sum, by mitigating inefficiencies in coaching models and shaping coaches' work, these logistics help optimize the enactment of a coaching model.

District and school leaders hold multiple responsibilities regarding managing the technical details of coaching, and it is also vital for these leaders to step back, reflecting on educators' receptivity to coaching as well as the environment for coaching and strategic improvement. In the following section, we discuss how leaders create and maintain a culture for coaching. When leaders improve the coaching culture, they not only enable coaches to engage in high-leverage coaching tasks, but they deepen the institutionalization of strategic, equity-centered coaching.

Make Coaching One with the Culture

Superintendents, principals, and other district leaders play key roles in centering coaching in the work of the organization and ensuring coaching matches their strategy. It is one thing to have a beautifully engineered plan that describes the district strategy and the actions designed to execute it, including coaching. It is another for leaders to demonstrate to everyone that they regard coaching as a vital enterprise. As such, we close by sharing multiple activities leaders can do to elevate coaching so that it matters for the system and its educators:

- Be seen with their own coaches.
- Share how coaching has helped them become better leaders.
- Arrange for presentations and/or reports on coaching to be given to the board.
- Explain publicly how coaching is integral to the work of the district.
- Include coaches on committees and in other leadership functions.
- Listen to coaches about successes and obstacles.
- Encourage leaders and teachers to engage in coaching.
- Encourage leaders and teachers to attend coaching training.

The objective here is to weave coaching into the normal operations of the district. We amplify that coaching should not be deemed an intervention of last resort for low-performing teachers or leaders, nor should it be seen as only for novice teachers and leaders, or for only the ambitious. Coaching should be a lever benefiting all educators. Further, school leaders should connect coaching with the strategy through the improvement routines that the district conducts (Stevenson & Lemons, 2021), so that it becomes baked into how the district does business. When coaching is tied to strategy and addressed by multiple leaders, it can take root and thrive, advancing equitable improvement.

TO MAKE COACHING MATTER

This chapter explicated the two-way street between coaching and strategy. We established how coaching is a potent component of strategy and how coaches can support aspects of the district improvement strategy. In the following lists, we offer recommendations for how district leaders, principals, and coaches can braid coaching with strategy. We encourage, again, treating the listed activities as a launching point for reflecting as an individual (or team, or organization) on the strategic-ness of coaching, and then developing contextualized plans for improving infrastructure and leadership to support strategic, equity-centered coaching.

District leaders should:

- create a coaching model connected to, and in service of, a strategy that connects the work of leaders, coaches, and teachers to the improvement of student learning;
- foster coherence across their organization, including a clear vision of the knowledge, skills, and dispositions that embody aspirations for students; a shared understanding of what high-quality instruction looks like; and a common commitment to coaching; and
- create opportunities to develop shared understandings of strategic priorities and coaching across their organization.

Principals should:

- discuss strategic priorities with coaches;
- explain to teachers how coaching functions in the service of strategy; and
- create conditions for coaches to focus on strategy in their work at the site.

Coaches should:

- hold a deep understanding of the strategic plan of their district and school(s);
- ask questions and request clarity regarding how their coaching should align with the strategic plan;

- conduct high-leverage coaching routines that address strategic priorities; and
- educate coachees about how coaching promotes strategic, equitable improvement.

This chapter delved into the benefits of constructing as well as instituting logical plans for the role of coaching in district improvement. Chapter 5 elevated the notion that coaching should cohere with strategy, so coaches promote organizational and individual learning. Here, we acknowledge that this form of strategic, equity-centered coaching is a complex craft. Attending to this complexity and embracing the notion that all educators can grow, Chapter 6 underscores the necessity of developing, supporting, and coaching coaches. Further, the next chapter delineates how system and school leaders can develop the knowledge, skills, and dispositions of coaches to support the enactment of coaching.

Building Capacity for Coaching

An investment in knowledge pays the best interest.

—Benjamin Franklin

Coaching—whether inside sports arenas, corporate headquarters, district central offices, or schools—rests on the assumption that everyone benefits from learning alongside a coach, because no one is perfect, and there is always room for improvement (Cox et al., 2014; Evered & Selman, 1989). Following this, coaches, too, as key capacity builders, benefit from professional development so they can improve. And, across our experiences, we have seen how coaches desire professional learning opportunities. Just as Chapter 2 presented what coaches should be doing to maximize the district's vision for coaching, here we present what coaches should learn so that they can best conduct their work. Importantly, not all this learning is limited to the nuts-and-bolts of how to coach, because coaching exists in a broader context and aims to effect change across multiple levels of the system. In addition, based upon the tenet that coaches, teachers, and other leaders need to understand what the district means by strategic, equitable coaching, we portray what professional learning should look like for a range of educators, permitting more productive engagement with their coach. Throughout this chapter, we describe how system and school leaders can design and foster professional learning opportunities for building capacity for coaches to help maximize coaching as an improvement lever.

Earlier chapters portrayed the landscape of coaching and how coaching can work toward equity-oriented goals—emphasizing that coaching is a component of strategy—and began discussing systems enabling coaching. These systems play a role in optimizing coaching by clearly framing what coaching entails and creating a robust culture for continuous improvement in which all educators are learning. In this chapter, we turn our attention to the systems, routines, and activities that build capacity for coaching. We address how to increase coaches' capacity and draw attention to increasing the capacity of district and school leaders for deploying coaching, and of multiple types of educators to be coached. Thus, we ask: How can coaches, administrators, and teachers learn about coaching? With groundings in theory, research, and practice, we share insights on professional learning for—and on—strategic coaching to reach equity-oriented goals. We encourage applying a coaching approach to ensure each coach develops skills and understandings regarding coaching itself. Finally, we remind reformers and leaders that it is vitally important to foster the learning of the system's coaches in a systemic, rather than individualized, way to build the team's capacity and promote organizational learning.

BACKGROUND ON GROWING AND SUSTAINING COACHES

Instructional coaches are frequently hired because they are skilled teachers who likely also shined as informal leaders, with the assumption that they can easily transmit their strengths to coach teachers. However, this situation puts coaches in the position of being a selected star, as well as the arbiter of quality, rather than as a colleague who works alongside teachers in pursuit of a common goal. Additionally, this situation prioritizes the content of coaching (e.g., how to differentiate math instruction, how to facilitate a writing workshop mini-lesson) over the coaching skills (e.g., providing feedback to a teacher on math instruction, facilitating a team meeting on writing assessment results). We contend, however, that coaches need to have opportunities to learn, practice, and refine coaching skills. This may seem glaringly obvious; however, there is a persistent mental model among many district leaders and boards of education that educators who were successful teachers and leaders will *ipso facto* be great coaches. This presumption underestimates the professional knowledge and skills that coaching requires as well as the amount of time needed to become a proficient coach.

Likewise, leadership coaches are often retired principals or superintendents who are hired because they were successful leaders. Our evaluation of leadership coaching for superintendents showed that new superintendents were very sensitive to the characteristics and skills of their coach. In particular, new superintendents noticed times when coaches seemed to be more interested in talking about what they did, or how they would have solved a problem—as opposed to being concerned about the issues the new superintendents currently faced, or supporting their thinking to address these challenges. And they noticed when their coaches did listen, asked constructive questions, challenged their assumptions, and helped them see options that they hadn't already thought of. This points to the importance of leadership coaches' skills as coaches in addition to their skills as former district leaders. Teaching successful educators to be coaches, therefore, frequently involves asking them to let go of mental models in which what matters in their coaching work is what they did—and what successes they had—when they held the role of their current coachee.

PROFESSIONAL DEVELOPMENT FOR COACHES

Perhaps the most obvious thing we can say here is that coaches need to be developed and supported on how to be coaches. There is no guarantee that educators in coaching roles have had any training on how to serve as a coach. This happens for several reasons. Sometimes there is a plan to hire coaches because a new budget line has been approved, but there is no plan to provide PD for the new coaches, so they learn on the job. This is not necessarily disastrous for new coaches because they were hired for having been successful teachers or leaders (the skills of teaching and leading certainly overlap with coaching), are quick thinkers and problem solvers, are reliable and conscientious, and have good collaboration and teamwork skills. But learning the craft of coaching without any formal grounding is slow and inefficient—trial and error takes a long time—and tends to lead to the entrenchment of pre-existing beliefs and schemas for what coaching looks like. Thus, becoming harder to unlearn if the district later generates a more explicit model for coaching or for official, common coaching PD.

Coaching hinges on the notion that, whether we are an Olympic-caliber gymnast, a novice principal, the mom of an 8-year-old, or a veteran high school biology teacher, we all benefit from opportunities to reflect, learn, and improve. So, beyond the initial coaching PD, when, where, and how do coaches—whether district-level math coaches, school improvement coaches, or leadership coaches—receive these opportunities so they can engage in their best work and contribute to strategic, equitable improvement? It is crucial that system and school leaders attend to coaches' opportunities for reflecting, learning, and improving. More specifically, leaders should design infrastructure that enables ongoing, contextualized professional development for coaches. In light of this, we describe major features of the content and format of PD with the potential to build coaches' capacity and enable systemwide learning on coaching. We argue that, to fully leverage coaching as an instrument for improvement, coach PD should address the purposes of coaching (as discussed in Chapter 3), elements of their specific coaching model, and routines of coaching (discussed in Chapter 2).

Foci of Coach Professional Development

To prepare and support coaches to conduct high-leverage coaching activities braided coherently with strategy and always targeting equity, school and district leaders should ensure the content of coach PD address the following three major domains: strategy and reform; the district's coaching model, including the expectations for how coaches should coach; and theories of learning/change. First, coach PD should demystify the district

Figure 6.1. Three foci of coach professional development.

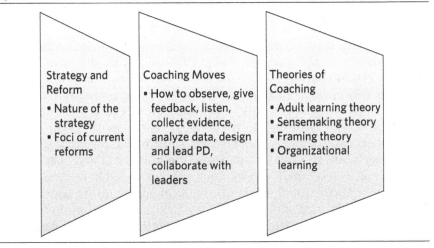

Strategy and Reform
• Nature of the strategy
• Foci of current reforms

Coaching Moves
• How to observe, give feedback, listen, collect evidence, analyze data, design and lead PD, collaborate with leaders

Theories of Coaching
• Adult learning theory
• Sensemaking theory
• Framing theory
• Organizational learning

and/or school strategy for equity and improvement while also explaining the pressures, regulations, and resources of the current policy environment. This sets the foundation for aligned coaching in the service of the strategy, vision, and equity. Foregrounding policy, equity, and big-picture goals, this PD equips coaches to serve as intermediaries. Second, PD should provide opportunities for coaches to learn about the conditions leaders should create for coaching, communication, and routines and methods of coaching. Third, coach PD should embed opportunities to gain knowledge regarding adult and organizational learning theory. This permits coaches to use learning theory lenses in their on-the-ground work. Below, we explain and illustrate how coach PD can address the three foci as shown in Figure 6.1, permitting shaping coaches' work as well as maximizing coaching as a reform instrument.

Professional Development on Equity, Strategy, and Reform

There are very few school districts that have a vision or mission that does not include the phrase "All students." As noted in Chapter 4, many districts are wrestling with equity-oriented reforms. As such, coaches are being asked to attend to issues of equity, because equity is part of the district's goals, is increasingly seen as what is happening *inside* classrooms, and changing what happens inside classrooms is increasingly seen as the domain of the coach. However, coaches do not typically have the same level of access or insight into district-level strategy as administrators do; they are not in "the room where it happens." We advocate that district leaders should rethink this, and invite coaches, who are frequently on the front line when it comes to enacting the district's strategy, into the room.

First, if coaches deeply understand district strategy and equity efforts, they will be better positioned to support and advance the strategy. Second, as coaches have insight into the workings of the district that few building and district leaders do, their voice in the creation of strategy is invaluable.

To enable coaches to engage in aligned work, leaders should design and facilitate PD for coaches in the context of the strategy, including current priorities, conceptions of equity, and equity-oriented approaches. Learning opportunities in these domains help coaches understand what the strategy is, how their work ties to the strategy, and how they can advance the strategy. For example, district leaders could plan a coach PD session in which they share strategy for increasing the number of marginalized students in higher-level math classes. Then coaches would have time and opportunity to discuss and flesh out the implications of this strategy for their coaching. Within this, some coaches may articulate how they already lead PD or support educators in ways coherent with the strategic plan, while other coaches may mention that they were uncertain about district priorities or that they had been pulled to work on other issues in their building. Notably, this activity would surface evidence regarding the enactment of the district plan as well as the nature of coaches' work across the district.

It is also beneficial for coach PD to provide in-depth information as well as engaging learning opportunities on current policies, reforms, and initiatives (Woulfin, 2018). When we refer to policy and reforms, this expansively includes educator evaluation systems, science curricula, reading intervention programs, discipline policy, and others. We have seen school-based improvement coaches, district level instructional coaches, and even leadership coaches who held spotty information about a reform or initiative, and, as a result, they struggled to communicate precisely about these reforms to teachers or leaders. In other settings, we have engaged with coaches who held deep understandings of major reforms, and they were able to skillfully modulate ideas on the reform with teachers and leaders and teach others about strands of the reform. If we seek coaches to advance deep changes in the direction of a reform, district and schools leaders need to arm them with information regarding particular reforms. Coaches need to know the policy so they can support it in their work with others. For this, leaders should set up learning opportunities so that coaches can gain knowledge and skills on policies—and to individually and collectively interpret policy messages—so they can implement it in their context in a manner to advance both strategy and equity (Coburn, 2001; Spillane et al., 2002).

Professional Development on Coaching Moves

Quality coach PD also addresses coaches' multifaceted work in facilitating adult learning and leading organizational improvement. This PD— on the how of coaching—seeks to build coaches' capacity to engage in high-leverage coaching practices, including observing teachers/leaders, providing feedback, and modeling practices (Russell et al., 2020). Thus, PD should unpack key coaching moves so that coaches hold the knowledge and skills necessary to advance change. Professional learning opportunities should increase coaches' knowledge of concepts of leadership and their competencies as leaders. For instance, coach PD could describe pillars of instructional leadership (i.e., prioritizing instruction; supporting instructional change), asking coaches to share how their work aligns to those pillars, providing learning opportunities on various pillars, and encouraging coaches to practice instructional leadership skills, including equity-oriented leadership moves (Rigby, 2014).

As addressed in Chapters 2 and 8, depending on the coaching model, the reform environment, and other conditions, coaches conduct a broad set of routines: from unit planning with teachers and providing feedback to novice principals to facilitating PD on EdTech and modeling culturally responsive instruction. So, sometimes we ask system leaders how coach PD addresses the nuts and bolts of coaching routines, and they respond vaguely that PD covered the new curriculum or introduced generic leadership strategies. This signals gaps in when, where, and how coaches gain capacity to carry out high-leverage coaching routines. Therefore, we propose coach PD should offer learning opportunities on how to carry out each coaching routine: from pre-observation meetings to planning conversations with principals. We also invite leaders to design and enact PD on how coaches can lead unit-planning meetings, communicate with principals, plan PD, and model various forms of instruction inside classrooms. Later in this chapter, we present what PD on specific coaching routines could entail to reflect tenets of adult learning, build coaches' capacity, and refine coaches' work routines.

By providing professional learning on each type of coaching routine, system leaders can not only raise the quality of key aspects of coaches' work and increase the likelihood coaches will conduct core routines, but boost the consistency of such coaching routines across the system. This means that reading coach post-observation conferences and principal supervisor walkthroughs would begin to look more similar across schools. Strategic, equity-centered coaching, as a lever, can be optimized when coaches across multiple schools learn about, use, and refine coaching routines. In particular, when routines stretch across schools, leaders can glean insights on strengths and areas of opportunity for the routine to work effectively to reach strategic, equitable goals across the system.

Similar to quality instruction for students that spirals content over time, coach PD over a school year should intentionally spiral through the routines of coaching, enabling coaches to experience multiple opportunities to learn about routines—from facilitating team meetings and having difficult conversations to setting a weekly calendar—rather than a single session on a routine. This spiraled design also ensures that PD addresses coaches' core work during different points in the school year. By spiraling these topics, leaders provide time and space for coaches to share how they enacted certain routines, successes and challenges emerging as they enacted routines, and reflections on how they might shift their enactment of routines in the future. Later in this chapter, we dive into the utility of coaches sharing their work in a venue resembling a community of practice (Wenger, 1998).

Additionally, coach PD should address communication strategies enabling coaches to transmit ideas on as well as motivate strategic, equitable change. To do so, coach PD can address how and why coaches communicate with teachers, leaders, and other constituents through various modalities, including (but not limited to): meetings, informal hallway conversations, email, and text messages. So, sessions would unpack the features of coach communication and offer reminders on benefits (and pitfalls) of various communication strategies. Moreover, this PD would expose coaches to models of clear, persuasive oral announcements, emails, and memos to different audiences. For example, a PD activity could ask coaches to draft a sample email or role-play making an announcement in a staff meeting in response to a scenario. Within this, leaders can refine coaches' skills in using technology to effectively communicate with leaders and teachers; sometimes an emoji in a text message is a fantastic way to convey ideas! In sum, addressing these communication strategies would assist in raising coaches' capacity to wield their informal authority to address a variety of ideas with a variety of actors.

PD must also confront how coaches' daily work collides with inequities, racism, and biases in order for them to attain strategic, equitable goals. Therefore, it is necessary for system leaders to design PD explicitly addressing how coaches should engage in courageous conversations with coachees and supervisors, confront racist and ableist language and approaches, and address coachee resistance to coaching on equity issues (Singleton, 2014). We underscore this PD would address coaches' roles and responsibilities when they see or hear inequity playing out in classrooms, offices, schools, and other venues.

As declared in Chapter 4, coaches' learning opportunities on inequity, institutionalized racism, and equity-centered coaching cannot be checked off by reading and discussing one article on anti-racist coaching, completing one activity to reflect on their privilege, or attending one webinar on courageous conversations. Instead, we emphasize leaders should design multiple, ongoing opportunities for coaches to learn about these critical and, oftentimes, challenging coaching practices. More specifically, leaders should create opportunities for coaches to practice and reflect on engaging in equity-centered coaching (e.g., reflecting on successes and realities in carrying out courageous conversations with other educators) and taking up anti-racist, anti-ableist coaching on a daily basis. Taken together, PD on the moves of coaching, including skillful, strategic communication on equity issues, functions to advance equity-centered coaching to advance strategy.

Professional Development on Theory

Certainly, coach PD should address the practical, logistical, and nitty-gritty details of policies, strategy and goals, and coaching routines, but it should also stretch to the theoretical level, providing learning opportunities on theories of adult learning and organizational change. These theories include lenses for coaches as change agents—with the potential to both explain and guide their work. Expanding points from Woulfin & Allen (2022), PD on the theoretical underpinnings of coaching supports coaches in making sharp, purposeful decisions regarding their foci and modes for coaching, connections to the wider system, and approaches to learning and educational improvement.

First, since coaches play key roles in delivering ongoing, contextualized learning to teachers and leaders, the tenets of adult learning theory provide useful lenses (Coburn & Woulfin, 2012). In particular, coach PD should introduce tenets of adult learning theory, including the conditions enabling adult learners to engage with learning opportunities and shift their beliefs and practices. One highlight is that adult learners benefit when they perceive new learning to be relevant to their situation and work. Thereby, adult learners, such as teachers or other coachees, can be hooked into learning in several ways—by matching coaching with current problems and by stating the why of coaching. In turn, coaches could make connections to those concepts and map out under what conditions their work aligns to those adult learning concepts. Coaches could share and describe how they currently address tenets of adult learning while facilitating meetings or coaching conversations.

Second, as coaches are responsible for leading change within complex organizations, concepts of organizational theory have relevance in—and for—their work. As such, district leaders should offer coach professional learning opportunities that showcase lenses from organizational theory, including coupling, sensemaking, and framing (Woulfin & Allen, 2022). Each of these theories includes concepts useful for describing facets of educational improvement, including challenges to change practice in substantive, coherent ways (Peurach et al., 2019). Each of these theories considers the relationship between ideas, people, and activities in an organizational context. Coupling theory focuses on the degree to which practices match formal rules and expectations. The concepts of coupling are useful for explaining how coaches' work ties to district strategy and reforms, and how coachees' work matches messaging from the coach.

Sensemaking theory focuses on how people interpret ideas or guidelines based upon their previous experiences and current collaborations and context; these interpretations steer organizational practices. In particular, sensemaking theory can illuminate how coachees make sense of coaching. Lastly, framing theory concentrates on how people communicate ideas and guidelines; that is, actors' frames strategically highlight some dimensions of an issue while blurring others. We note the concepts of framing have utility for explaining the benefits of clear, consistent, motivational communication from a coach in improvement efforts.

To link theory with coaches' work, coaches should be invited to reflect on how those concepts surface in their work. For example, after developing understandings of coupling theory, coaches could map the ways that they tightly couple some branches of district policy in their work while loosely coupling other dimensions of district policy. In turn, as a team, coaches may realize how their work is strongly linked to district guidelines on formative assessments, but only loosely reflects tenets of culturally sustaining instruction. Next, coaches would create plans for altering the coupling of strategic priorities to strengthen the coherence between their daily practices and big picture goals. In this way, coaches would build capacity on applications of organizational theory to refine their work in the organization, contributing to strategic, equitable organizational change.

DESIGN FEATURES OF COACH PROFESSIONAL DEVELOPMENT

Above, we put forth a mighty agenda with multiple strands for coach PD. Now, we shift attention to the nature and format of this PD to make coaching matter. Here, we remind reformers and leaders that the *pedagogy* of coach PD matters for whether and how it yields learning for coaches and, ultimately, translates into changes in coaches' work to help reach system-level goals (Desimone et al., 2002; Garet et al., 2001; Woulfin, 2017). That is, the format and activities of PD on district strategy and policies, coaching routines and communication, and theories of learning and change will influence coaches' engagement in PD, their responses to PD, and the potential for this PD to strengthen the coaching system. If leaders seek to change coaches' work and maximize their coaching model, it is vital to construct continuous learning opportunities that go beyond PowerPoint presentations, email announcements, disconnected workshops, and book clubs on coaching. Here, we unpack promising structures for coach PD and then we depict learning activities fruitful for improving coaching. As summarized in Table 6.1, we describe how common plus specialized PD, PLCs, and coaching expand coaches' professional learning to raise their readiness to conduct strategic, equity-centered coaching.

Table 6.1. Affordances and concrete examples of design features of coach professional development.

Design Feature	Affordances	Example
Common plus specialized	• Coaches across a system develop common understandings of equity and strategy. • Coaches across a system engage in collective professional learning on common coaching routines. • Specialized coaches gain access to ideas and information related to their target area.	• Elementary and secondary ELA and math coaches attend instructional leadership PD sessions at four points during the school year to encounter common messaging on district strategy, high-quality instructional leadership, and high-leverage coaching routines.
Professional learning community	• Coaches build networks, reduce isolation. • Coaches learn from each other's experiences and offer constructive feedback to promote improvement. • System leaders can obtain evidence to engage in continuous improvement on their coaching model.	• Math coaches meet two times per month to share evidence on their work, analyze data, and co-develop tools to guide their coaching.
Coaching	• Coaches encounter contextualized, tailored learning opportunities. • Coaches are supported within their context.	• The District's ELA director models a principal–coach strategy plan check-in meeting for a novice ELA coach.

Common Plus Specialized Professional Development. To advance strategic, equity-centered coaching, there are benefits to common as well as specialized PD for coaches working in a system. We have collaborated with districts where elementary literacy, school turnaround, and principal leadership coaches rarely engage in common PD; they are rarely in the room together. As a result, they use entirely different routines, tools, and communication strategies which may raise teacher/leader stress and, even more importantly, detract from strategic objectives and reduce the potential of coaching to foster change. To counter this, we take the stance that coaches concentrating on different foci within a single system should engage in shared PD on facets of coaching.

Returning to the example of a district who employs elementary literacy, turnaround, and principal leadership coaches, these distinct sets of coaches should experience some common professional learning opportunities on the overarching goal for systemic improvement and the district's broad vision for coaching. In particular, district leaders could offer PD for these three types of coaches on shared routines and terminology for their coaching, such as walkthroughs and equity-centered conversations. The common PD prepares coaches—whether a literacy coach working with 3rd-grade teachers or a leadership coach working with high school principals—to engage in consistent coaching routines, use consistent language, and set expectations with coachees. In turn, these consistent threads would serve to foster a culture for coaching within which coachees see and hear common approaches to coaching for strategic, equitable improvement.

During this common, integrated coach PD, each type of coach would be encouraged to identify points of divergence; that is, how are feedback conversations different for literacy and leadership coaches, and how can they explain these differences in coaching structures and practices to their particular coachee? This would help support a turnaround coach working in a middle school to introduce how their coaching will devote attention to schoolwide data-use routines and intervention programs in contrast to the literacy coach's focus on the pedagogy of reading and writing instruction in PK–3 classrooms. Importantly, during common coach PD, coaches and system leaders can also explore the ways coaching can remain supportive, rather than being deemed as onerous or punitive by coachees. For this, we encourage drafting plans regarding who coaches will concentrate on at different points in the year and considering how to reduce the burden of being coached. Thus, coaches would work collaboratively to reduce the too-muchness of coaching, particularly for educators expected to engage with multiple coaches simultaneously.

At the same time, different types of coaches with different foci benefit from holding expertise in their specialty area. It remains important to build coaches' capacity in specialized ways so that they hold the knowledge and skills related to their specific domain and for coaching in their specific domain. For example, literacy coaches benefit from in-depth professional learning opportunities on the literacy curriculum to be prepared to observe teachers' enactment of the curriculum, and principal coaches benefit from in-depth professional learning opportunities on the system's vision for leadership and on techniques for engaging with current principals to be prepared to work effectively with school leaders.

With the objective of supporting multiple, specific types of coaching, system leaders should design and enact coach PD that provides time for specialized learning opportunities tailored to their coaches' foci. In effect, the PD system should include common and "break-out" venues, literally or metaphorically, such that coaches encounter a shared set of learning opportunities with common messages on strategy, equity, and leadership and a specialized set of learning opportunities with targeted messages on the coaching of specific content areas and the nuts-and-bolts of reforms. A concrete example would be a district math coach attending some PD sessions with elementary literacy coaches and high school turn-around coaches to learn about the district's vision for coaching and techniques for communicating with teachers about improvement efforts. But this math coach would also engage in PD sessions with their team of mathematics coaches to learn about the district's adopted mathematics instructional materials, how to engage in real-time coaching on mathematics instruction, and how to design more effective mathematics PD for teachers.

Coach Professional Learning Community. Mirroring how teachers and principals engage in productive professional learning activities, form networks, and gain professional support within a PLC (Blase & Blase, 2003; DuFour, 2004), we propose that system leaders adopt the PLC model to build coaches' capacity. A coach PLC would assemble structures and enact routines and practices to help form a trusting network of coaches who work collaboratively to achieve better system-level results. Therefore, a coach PLC is a space plus a set of enacted routines encouraging collaboration across a team of coaches to promote learning among coaches and across the system. Importantly, the routines of a coach PLC include those guiding coaches to engage in cycles of inquiry and continuous improvement regarding their coaching.

We articulate that PLCs are a promising model for developing and supporting coaches as key actors to foster strategic, equitable change. First, the PLC model elevates coaches as professionals, valuing their existing knowledge and skills and aiming to promote continuous improvement. As such, a coach PLC treats coaches as the local experts who carry out strategic, equity-centered improvement work. Therefore, the coach PLC becomes a robust model for how coaches themselves may organize another PLC with teams of their own coachees to provide professional support and promote contextualized learning.

Second, the PLC model carves out time and space for coaches to transparently share their work, obtain ideas for improvement from their coach-colleagues, and raise questions about reforms and conditions. We have observed coach PLCs in California and Connecticut in which coaches shared resources and tools with other coaches in their districts, and asked tough questions about current district priorities and future initiatives. Moreover, when system leaders facilitate a coach PLC, they are able to gather information on the intricacies of coaching, including coaches' strengths and gaps in current conditions for coaching. For example, system leaders may hear how coaches experience resistance to learning walks or lack time to engage in lesson rehearsal activities with novice teachers. System leaders, in turn, can respond by adapting messaging and supports for these particular dimensions of coaching. Once again, we have observed and supported district leaders to use information from the dialogue in coach PLC sessions to refine their coaching model. In one case, a district director noticed coaches repeatedly mentioned limited opportunities to communicate with principals. Based upon this, the director launched PD for principals on how to engage with coaches.

In sum, a coach PLC is fruitful for promoting individual as well as organizational learning. This is due to how the community of coaches not only expands a coach's network, and their individual knowledge and skills, but enables system-level, or organizational, learning on improvement efforts.

Coaching for Coaches. By this point, you may be thinking that this ongoing, coherent, targeted, and contextualized PD looks and sounds a lot like coaching itself! We agree, and, yes, coaches deserve—and benefit from—coaching. Feedback, observations, modeling, and other coaching practices provide tailored learning opportunities to raise the coaches' knowledge and skills. Moreover, when coaches themselves are coached, they experience the nuances of coaching, helping them gain a sense of successes and barriers in coaching as well as the emotional dimensions of being coached. When coaches are coached, they are better able to put themselves in the shoes of their coachees.

In this chapter, we encourage a coaching approach to develop coaches' knowledge, skills, and dispositions for advancing strategic, equitable change. We point to the role of system leaders in ensuring coaches are coached (Mangin & Dunsmore, 2015; Woulfin, 2020). Specifically, system leaders should consider who will coach various coaches in their system. For example, an associate superintendent could coach leadership coaches, and the director of ELA could coach reading coaches. When school and system leaders coach coaches, it provides them vital support, makes dimensions of coaching more explicit, indicates the system's prioritization of coaching and continuous improvement, and propels coaches' learning so that they are better prepared to carry out coaching. We have been impressed by districts in which leaders proudly assert: Everyone here has a coach! Everyone is always being coached so that they can grow and thrive! These mantras announce that coaching is a priority, that system leaders fully understand the power of coaching to promote adult learning and PD, and that they are committed to framing coaching in a positive, supportive light.

To clarify the nature of coaching for coaches, we share the following two examples. In Rose District, coaching coaches entails system leaders enacting coaching routines during their engagement with coaches. For example, the district's director of mathematics shadows each math coach and then provides feedback on the coach's work at multiple points in the school year. Through this, the director shares evidence with the coach on their use of time and then generates strategies for improving their use of time to engage in focal math coaching routines. On occasion, this director models routines, including real-time coaching, for coaches at their sites.

As another example, this district's chief of academics facilitates leadership goal-setting meetings for new principal supervisors in his district. Through this facilitation, the chief of academics models key steps in leadership coaching and then engages in reflective conversations to highlight key principles/moves for coaching school leaders. Across the two examples, the elbow-to-elbow work, analysis of evidence, and discussion of coaching routines deepen adult learning for coaches to strengthen their coaching skills and efforts. We also point to how the system's structures and norms enable coaches to be coached in a purposeful way to ensure coachees hold the knowledge and skills to work toward strategic, equitable change.

EVERYBODY'S GOTTA LEARN ABOUT COACHING

The previous section of this chapter depicted the content and format promoting robust, supportive coach PD. This PD has the potential to shape coaches' work. We have seen, however, that ongoing, contextualized, networked, engaging PD for coaches is beneficial, but it is not sufficient for strategic, equitable coaching. If highly prepared and well-supported coaches encounter misunderstandings or resistance from coachees, it can become difficult for coaches to engage in high-leverage coaching activities, and, in turn, the coaching model will flounder. Thus, to counter these blockages, systems also need to raise and improve principals' and teachers' awareness and knowledge of coaching. In the following sections, we explore the effects of PD for principals, other leaders, and teachers on coaching. We sketch out learning opportunities for those supervising coaches, and those being coached by coaches, so that they fully understand the guidelines, routines, and activities of strategic, equity-centered coaching.

Professional Development for Principals on Coaching. System leaders seeking to refine and optimize coaching can take steps to build the capacity of principals regarding dimensions of coaching. In the following list, we outline the importance of principals engaging in learning opportunities on:

- system-level goals for coaching, including the expectation that coaching ties to strategy and advances equity;
- components of the coaching model;
- what coaches' high-leverage practices look and sound like;
- conditions enabling coaching in their building; and
- activities permitting effective collaboration with coaches.

We encourage system leaders to design and facilitate PD for principals on the purpose and nature of coaching in their system. These opportunities would lay out how the system is defining coaching, how coaching intertwines with district and school strategic plans, and how coaching serves to advance equity-oriented goals. We highlight that system leaders should expose principals to ideas regarding what high-leverage coaching entails, including what key coaching routines (e.g., walkthroughs, feedback conversations, facilitating team meetings) look and sound like, as well as when and where those routines should take place. System leaders should also elevate the principles and practices of equity-centered coaching so that principals have concrete understandings regarding the intersection of coaching and equity reforms. Consequently, principals would gain insights as to the rationale for and value of coaching and, ultimately, better support coaches plus their coaching to reach strategic, equity-oriented goals.

By expanding principals' understanding of how to create positive conditions for coaching and supporting the ongoing growth of coaches, PD for principals on coaching would raise their instructional leadership competencies in numerous ways. First, PD could provide ideas and information related to how principals set aside time and space for coaching to occur. For instance, the PD could include activities in which principals analyze the school's calendar and schedule to determine when coaches can meet with teachers as well as how to adapt collaboration guidelines to enable the full implementation of the coaching model.

This PD could also operationalize how principals can collaborate with coaches. For example, principal PD could include activities for principals to role-play planning meetings with coaches or practice providing feedback after co-observing with a coach. In this manner, principals would develop strategies and skills for communicating with coaches about issues to ensure coaching revolves around strategic priorities. In turn, principals would be better prepared to discuss school goals and foci with their coach to promote aligned coaching efforts. Finally, this PD could support school leaders in understanding how to clearly introduce their coach to teachers and to thoughtfully frame the objectives of coaching for teachers. Within this, we urge system leaders to explain how these introductions set the stage for teachers' engagement with coaches. These introductions also preserve coaches' time so that they can more efficiently launch into the core routines of strategic, equity-centered coaching instead of dumping time into introductions and activities defining who they are, why they are working in a particular school or with particular teachers, and what coaching will involve.

Professional Development for Educators on Coaching. We caution that if coachees lack a clear understanding of the coaching model, its strategic objectives, and components of coaches' work, coaching may feel like a burden—or yet another initiative. If educators possess muddy understandings of coaching, they may fail to view it as an instrument for reaching strategic, equity-oriented goals. We underscore that, since coaching is relatively new and holds many definitions, teachers interpret coaching in different ways and may have limited, or faulty, access to ideas on the what, how, and why of coaching. Therefore, teachers, too, should engage in professional learning opportunities on the why, how, what, where, and when of their systems coaching model. Mirroring facets of leader PD, teacher PD on coaching should address:

- system-level goals for coaching, including the expectation that coaching ties to strategy and advances equity;
- components of the coaching model;
- what coaches' high-leverage practices look and sound like;
- conditions enabling coaching in their building; and
- activities permitting effective collaboration with coaches.

By encountering messages on the underlying purposes of coaching, the components of the coaching model, and the conditions supporting teachers and coaches to work together, teachers and leaders can construct shared schemas of coaching and embrace coaching. In turn, if educators make sense of coaching structures and practices in aligned ways, coaches can conduct high-leverage coaching activities, including observing instruction and providing feedback, with fewer obstacles from current and possible coachees. Here, we lean on the notion that coachees sometimes say "no" to coaching not because they wish to avoid working with a specific coach or due to resistance to being observed, but because they lack a full understanding of the purpose and expectations of coaching.

Stemming from these points on the necessity of teachers understanding the purpose, targets, and tools of coaching, we offer the reminder that teachers should experience PD that clarifies how coaching is braided together with and uplifts the strategic plan. Addressing misconceptions related to individualized, haphazard coaching, this could frame coaches' work as serving to advance strategic, equitable change. Additionally, this PD should depict various features of coaching—with definitions of routines, examples of what routines would entail, and space for teachers to share questions, reflections, and feedback on each routine. In sum, this PD provides a foundation for teachers to partner with coaches so that coaches can jump into their work and the vision and mission of the system's coaching model becomes realized. Finally, PD should address how teachers can partner and communicate with their coach. For instance, teachers could generate ideas on what to ask coaches to observe or how to follow up so that a coach models specific practices in their classroom. Through these activities, teachers would gain skills for collaborating with—and even coaching up—coaches. In turn, this enables teachers to learn how to get the most out of coaching. Taken together, when teachers gain capacity as coachees, this assists in maximizing coaching in the school and system.

TO MAKE COACHING MATTER

In this chapter, we explained the role of professional development in supporting the implementation of strategic, equity-centered coaching. Then we described design features of professional learning opportunities for coaches plus teachers and other leaders on the coaching model, its routines, and broad objectives. In the following list, we share potential action steps for district leaders, principals, and coaches to promote capacity building on coaching. These recommendations are rooted in the idea that fully leveraging strategic, equity-centered coaching requires learning. Further, the recommendations are based in the idea that clarity around expectations, coupled with ongoing support, advances change aligned with the coaching model.

District leaders should:

- design and facilitate professional development for coaches, principals, and teachers on the coaching model and how to engage with coaches;
- provide coaching to coaches to practice coaching strategies and skills; and
- collect and analyze evidence on strengths and gaps in learning opportunities for coaches.

Principals should:

- engage in PD regarding the nature of the coaching model and how to support coaches;
- support coaches so that they continue developing as professionals; and
- build teachers' understanding of how and why to engage in coaching.

Coaches should:

- engage in ongoing, contextualized professional development on priorities, leadership, and coaching routines; and
- openly share feedback on learning needs and opportunities to system and school leaders.

This chapter shed light on the role of educator capacity building in furthering strategic, equity-centered coaching. We depicted design features of engaging, contextualized, coherent approaches to professional learning associated with the structures and practices of coaching. Further, Chapter 6 pointed to the necessity of providing PD on coaching to multiple types of leaders and teachers—rather than solely coaches—to strengthen the implementation of coaching in addition to improving coaches' work. In Chapter 7, we direct further attention toward the improvement of coaching, and how strategic, equity-centered coaching fosters improvement. Drawing on concepts of continuous improvement, the next chapter puts forth claims about—and includes illustrations of—how coaching supports educators to learn how to improve.

Continuous Improvement in and Through Coaching

The U.S. education system is notorious for changing again and again and again (Cuban, 1990). Educational organizations are always evolving, striving to improve, and attempting to function as learning organizations (Bryk et al., 2015). Rising to face these challenges, scholars, reformers, and leaders have elevated the principles and practices of continuous improvement (Mehta et al., 2022; Yurkofsky et al., 2020). These scholars and practitioners underscore that change often occurs in incremental steps, that educators should listen and learn from challenges as well as successes in implementation, and that refining practices can build toward organizational improvement (Bryk et al., 2015). Further, they have shed light on the role of various leaders in structuring and carrying out continuous improvement.

Across the education field, continuous improvement (CI) has become nearly as popular as coaching. Yet, when we ask superintendents and principals what continuous improvement looks like in their organization, they often describe creating and checking school improvement plans based on the previous year's accountability data, conducting instructional rounds, and scheduling PLC or data team meetings. It appears, therefore, district and school leaders expect that engaging in these processes is sufficient to make a claim that CI is taking place in their schools and districts. In contrast, we assert it is essential to look deeply into what it means to engage in continuous improvement and attend to how coaching plays a role in CI.

Coaching and CI are interlinked because, ultimately, coaching not only teaches people how to get better, it also teaches people how to get better at getting better. This premise—of getting better at getting better—is at the heart of continuous improvement (Bryk et al., 2015). Based upon this, this chapter explores key ideas and actions for linking coaching with continuous improvement, including:

- how continuous improvement is embedded in coaching; and
- how coaching can be incorporated into continuous improvement of a district's strategy.

Given our experience that districts and schools struggle with continuous improvement, we note that devoting attention to how both *coaching* as a model for learning and change, and *coaches* as professionals skilled in facilitating learning and change, can contribute to continuous improvement. On the one hand, coaching models can reflect principles of CI and ask coaches to target on CI objectives. On the other hand, as coaches support the thinking and experimentation that goes into the professional growth of teachers and leaders, it makes sense that they would be involved in continuous improvement. For this to occur, coaches must engage with groups as well as individuals, and even to an entire school or district.

We also argue it is necessary to attend to how coaching contributes to organizational improvement. District and school leaders—and coaches themselves—should collect and use evidence on the enactment of coaching because evaluating coaching is a vital step to continuously improve it. In other words, leaders should determine whether and how coaching is making a difference so that they can ensure coaching matters.

WHAT DO WE MEAN BY CONTINUOUS IMPROVEMENT?

Continuous improvement is better than delayed perfection.

—Mark Twain

Continuous improvement is not a new idea, and it has been applied in multiple sectors. The concept has been traced back to the work of Shewhart and Deming on manufacturing and management methods (Petersen, 1999). Both advanced the notion that the best way to improve the quality of a product is to improve the process that creates it. This idea may sound like a truism, or perhaps too obvious to bother pointing out. However, the U.S. education system has tended to focus on outcomes at the expense of process—witness the emphasis on holding schools accountable for outcomes during the era of No Child Left Behind, and the emphasis on holding teachers accountable for student achievement during the era of Race to the Top. Many districts adopted similar approaches, asking schools to adopt ambitious goals for increasing test scores, without providing requisite supports for strengthening the work that, in actuality, produces those scores.

Continuous improvement is most often represented as a cycle such as Plan-Do-Study-Act (PDSA), shown in Figure 7.1. We summarize four stages of continous improvement (Bryk et al., 2015):

1. Plan: Generating a theory of action for how a problem or challenge might be addressed. Creating a plan for trying to improve.

Figure 7.1. Four stages of continuous improvement related to a problem of practice.

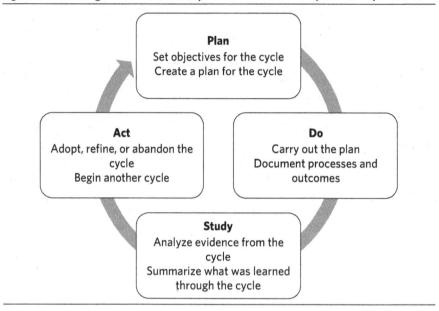

2. Do: Putting the theory of action to the test by performing some kind of experiment.
3. Study: Collecting and analyzing data on the results of the experiment.
4. Act: Using that data to refine the theory.

Over the last several years, inspired by developments in continuous improvement in health care (Bryk et al., 2015; Langley et al., 2009;) and the rise in popularity of design thinking, educational organizations and leaders have embraced continuous improvement. There are now multiple resources, grounded in improvement science, that can support the study, design, and implementation of problems and solutions related to improving education. In this more comprehensive portrayal of CI, the PDSA cycle is only one component of the improvement process; see Figure 7.2. As portrayed in multicolored diagrams with multiple arrows, CI processes involve multiple people, including coaches, conducting multiple steps to foster collective learning and organizational change. For example, leaders use logic models and driver diagrams to develop a shared theory of improvement and then generate evidence-based, user-centered ideas to enact and test in their context. Due to the complexity of CI and level of coordination necessary to enact CI, it is vital to attend to the structures and conditions providing a foundation for CI.

Figure 7.2. Map of broader continuous improvement processes.

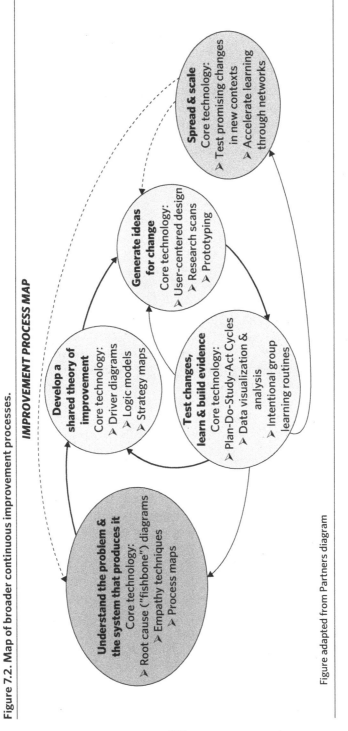

IMPROVEMENT PROCESS MAP

Spread & scale
Core technology:
➤ Test promising changes in new contexts
➤ Accelerate learning through networks

Generate ideas for change
Core technology:
➤ User-centered design
➤ Research scans
➤ Prototyping

Develop a shared theory of improvement
Core technology:
➤ Driver diagrams
➤ Logic models
➤ Strategy maps

Test changes, learn & build evidence
Core technology:
➤ Plan-Do-Study-Act Cycles
➤ Data visualization & analysis
➤ Intentional group learning routines

Understand the problem & the system that produces it
Core technology:
➤ Root cause ("fishbone") diagrams
➤ Empathy techniques
➤ Process maps

Figure adapted from Partners diagram

CREATING THE CONDITIONS FOR CONTINUOUS IMPROVEMENT

While it is possible to think of continuous improvement as a set of tools and protocols, these will have limited utility unless broader structures and other conditions are in place (Stevenson & Weiner, 2020). Due to this, we turn attention to conditions enabling CI (Mehta et al., 2022; Yurkofsky, 2022). First, engagement in continuous improvement rests on certain shared understandings about the direction the district is headed, and the role of coaching in supporting that direction, which was the subject of Chapter 5. As such, continuous improvement efforts are difficult and inefficient at best, and frustrating and dead-end at worst, without agreement around the following:

- What the district is working toward (vision), the strategy and/ or theory of action for how this is to be accomplished, and where coaching fits in supporting the strategy (see Chapter 5).
- How coaching is to be practiced in support of the strategy (see Chapters 2, 4, and 8).
- The conditions that leaders are expected to create in support of strategy and coaching (see Chapters 4, 5, 6, and 8).

Second, educators' sensemaking of CI affects how they implement it. Educators who think about continuous improvement as a set of tools and protocols, or an event they have to find time for, are much less likely to be able to take advantage of its potential than those who see it as a way of thinking about their work that they employ all the time. In contrast, if CI becomes integrated into all aspects of the organization and becomes deemed "the way things work around here," it is likely more deeply implemented. We share a few examples of the range of orientations toward CI from districts with different experiences with, and stances toward, CI. And we encourage reflecting on how you have seen these modes of CI and how to apply a learning versus compliance orientation for CI. That is, how can districts and their coaches embed principles and practices of CI into multiple structures and routines? What else could help bridge coaching and CI?

- Rule followers: Teachers and leaders treat continuous improvement as something that they "ought" to be doing, or do not have the capacity to enact fully because educators in the organization don't understand it and don't have the skills, or see continuous improvement as an add-on, parallel to but separate from the core work of the organization. In this scenario, continuous improvement is not enacted, or it is enacted superficially, because of gaps in understandings of how to engage in CI.

- Assimilators: Leaders think that they are "doing continuous improvement" because they have annual plans that specify goals and the collection of data, and because teachers are meeting monthly in data teams or PLCs. Districts in this scenario have made the resource commitment for teachers to collaborate regularly, but not for teachers and leaders to fully understand the deeper underpinnings of continuous improvement. They are not, therefore, "doing continuous improvement" at all, but they are happy with their situation.

- Delegators: Leaders think that they are "doing continuous improvement" because they have provided training and templates for teachers to meet regularly to study their student achievement data, with the tacit theory of action that if they study their data, they will make appropriate adjustments to their instruction. This is a far too limited view of CI, because there is very little support for the implementation of changes based on the analysis of data. Also, all too often in this scenario, leaders think that CI applies to teachers but not to them.

- Improvers: Districts where teachers and leaders have the knowledge, skills, and dispositions to think in terms of continuous improvement, will weave the approach throughout their work, whether or not someone gives them a template to follow. The dispositions that are most closely aligned with the practice of continuous improvement are: a propensity to engage in disciplined inquiry; adoption of a learning stance; taking a systems perspective; seeking the perspective of others; a willingness to act; and persistence beyond initial improvement attempts.

The improvement process can happen at many scales within a school district. As we mentioned, many leaders associate CI with mesolevel, teacher data teams. And, indeed, the notion that teachers would organize and collaborate around researching and improving their own practice is one way of enacting CI. But CI also exists at the macrolevel, involving improving the organization as a whole, or working to ensure the organization *gets better at getting better*. Finally, CI unfolds at the microlevel, including when a coach engages in planning, studying, doing, and acting with their coachee(s).

Importantly, coaching can be melded into the following interlocking cycles of improvement:

1. Teachers are working on a cycle of improvement centered on their instructional practice, supported by coaches.
2. Coaches are working on a cycle of improvement involving their practice of coaching.

3. District and school leaders are working on a cycle of improvement centered on their leadership practice, supported by coaches.
4. District and school teams are working on improving the organization's strategy for improvement, and coaches are included in these teams.

Continuous improvement means that improvement should be, well, continuous. The potential power of the cycle of continuous improvement is in the use of data as feedback to improve a strategy or one of its components. The speed of that cycle matters. When it comes to the usefulness of feedback, timeliness matters—the size of the improvement is correlated with the quality and the frequency of the feedback. When you think about it that way, it becomes obvious that an annual improvement cycle does not involve much improvement. Nevertheless, it is not unusual for CI to be performed as an annual event in which schools set goals for student achievement based on a best-guess increase compared with the previous year's results. Then they conduct a languid swoop through the four PDSA stages, resulting in a low degree of CI implementation.

COACHING FOR CONTINUOUS IMPROVEMENT

As discussed earlier in this chapter, we view coaching as reflecting principles of CI. In particular, coaches' work is constituted of looking at evidence, creating improvement plans, learning together, and discussing how change unfolded and what additional changes could be beneficial. In the following sections, we unpack what key coaching routines might sound like when the coach is taking up the principles and practices of CI.

Clarifying Goals

Coaches play an important role in clarifying goals; this assists for planning in CI. Coaching conversations should begin with clarity about the goal: What are you trying to accomplish? This is perhaps the most deceptively simple of all questions in coaches' work. It is not as easy to answer as might be expected. First, the coachee may not be completely clear on what they are trying to achieve, or if the client is a group, there may be disagreement among the members. Also, what the client says in response to this question may already have some assumptions built into it. For example, we worked with a principal who responded that their goal was for teachers to turn in lesson plans every Friday. When we probed, her theory was that if teachers were required to turn in their plans, then they would plan their lessons more meticulously, and their questioning during instruction would be more rigorous. When we asked what she would do if the lesson plans were not of high quality, she was stumped; it just had not occurred to her that that might be the case. And so, the question about what the client is trying to accomplish leads to other questions about what their ideal is, the assumptions they hold about what is causing the problem they are trying to solve, and suppression of their initial assumptions about what will get them to their target.

Many of the educators we work with associate coaching with post-observation conferences, and are accustomed to starting those conversations with some variation of: "How do you think it [the lesson/leadership work observed] went?" They tend to be shocked when we begin, instead, with: "So, what would you like to get out of this conversation?" We use that opening for three reasons: First, if the client says that they think it went wonderfully and the students got a lot out of it and we disagree, then we are already having to navigate a conflict and the conversation has just started! Second, we want to communicate that the conversation has a specific purpose—we are here to work toward improvement, not to chat, or check in. Third, we want a measure for whether the conversation was helpful; it is impossible to know that unless we know the target we are trying to reach. Frequently, the question about the goal for the conversation has to be repeated; the client starts talking about what is foremost in their mind, and it is easy to start chatting. As such, there is a discipline involved in listening to what the coachee says and making sure that they answer the goal question to create a launching point for the coaching conversation and to foster CI.

Understanding the Problem

Coaching conversations that reflect CI involve studying and understanding what the problem is. Coachees often share assumptions about their problem of practice, its root causes, which solution will work, what they can and cannot do, and what other people will think or do. Within this, the coach's role is to ask probing questions about where the client is relative to the goal. Here the coach is trying to ascertain what the client knows about the combination of factors that is causing the current situation. Together, they can study the issue.

As mentioned earlier in this book, it is here that we are most likely to hear "solutionitis." Bryk et al. (2015) use this term to describe the tendency to choose a course of action based on confidence that the problem is already known and the solution is obvious. Frequently, the client's preferred solution is disguised as a statement about the problem, such as "the problem is we don't have enough counselors"; "the problem is the teachers don't want to give up the extra planning time"; or "the problem is that the curriculum is too cumbersome." The coach, then, must nudge the client toward collecting additional information that will provide a clearer understanding of the set of issues causing the problem. This could include conducting a root cause analysis together to study the problem. It could also simply involve asking: "How do you know what's behind the current situation, and how could you find out?" For this, coaches play a central role in encouraging using and even generating data to better understand problems.

As coaches engage in CI, we elevate the importance of collecting and using street data (Safir & Dugan, 2021). This form of data includes information about the experience of those who have first-hand knowledge of the issue at hand; it is often obtained by simply asking them. The coach might use a variety of tools to help the client make sense of the data they have collected and to provide the coach a better understanding of where they might intervene. For instance, fishbone diagrams organize collected data results to show what factors are contributing to the problem. And a process map or a flowchart are strong for visualizing multiple steps between cause(s) and effect.

Developing a Theory of Action

As mentioned before, we see clients frequently disguising their preferred solution as a problem, and both may be incomplete or unknown. To address this issue, we assist clients in generating multiple possible options for action, helping them see that it is almost always the case that they have several choices for what to do next, and making it clearer to them that they can choose among alternatives that have various upsides and downsides. Developing a theory of action involves coming up with a hypothesis about what change will cause improvement. For this, coaches should ask lots of questions, many of which are the same as or connected to the questions in the Improvement Process Map, including:

- Can you clarify the goal for me?
- How do you know that's the real problem; could something else be going on?
- What assumptions are you making?
- What other options do you have?
- What change do you think will make the largest difference?
- How will you know?
- How will other people and/or other parts of the organization be affected?

As Edmondson and Verdin (2017) point out, sometimes you can only know whether your change idea is a good one by trying it out, because data about whether a change is successful can only be gathered through implementation.

Generating Possible Actions

It is quite tempting for people to think that they know what needs to be done to solve a particular problem: if only those teachers had higher expectations; if only leaders spent more time in classrooms; if only the district hired more science coaches; if only the coaches were better at having courageous conversations. The solutions that are most obvious to educators, whatever their role, almost always involve what *other* educators should be doing differently. As such, a vital role of coaches for supporting continuous improvement is to (1) prompt educators and teams to frame solutions in a way that puts them at the center of, rather than adjacent to, or the beneficiary of, a possible solution; (2) to consider a range of possible change ideas rather than assuming that the solution is easy and obvious; (3) to choose a change idea to try based on an assessment of how much impact can be created from a reasonable amount of effort; (4) to implement a change idea that is easily and quickly tested; and (5) to use data collected on implementation to make further improvements.

This is precisely why coaching functions as a driver of continuous improvement. That is, since a fundamental tenet of coaching is that coaches insist that their clients list several options and weigh them, rather than acting on the first thing that comes to mind, coaching encourages exploring multiple facets of an issue. Further, coaches can ask follow-up questions, such as: Which option would give you the most information about what's causing the problem? If you tried this, what do you think would happen next? Is there anyone else you could involve at this point? In these ways, coaches can be involved in generating alternative solutions and creating plans reflecting CI.

Test, Learn, and Adjust

It is one thing to decide what to do, and another to actually do it, especially when the action carries some risk of annoying someone, being judged negatively, or simply not getting the desired outcome. Coaches provide boosts for the action phase of CI, such as: role-playing a conversation that the client anticipates will be awkward or difficult; framing a change as an experiment rather than a permanent commitment; and talking through the potential risks to mitigate or prepare for. Here, we offer the reminder that CI requires patience and tenacity. Coaches can model both. Coaches also play a role in holding individuals and teams to a soft accountability of keeping track of what they said they would do. In sum, several strands of coaching promote the "act" phase of CI.

ROUTINES OF CONTINUOUS IMPROVEMENT

A major difference we see between districts that substantively take up the principles and practices of continuous improvement and those that do not is that the former districts employ routines ensuring that continuous improvement is the deeply institutionalized, taken-for-granted, normal way that work unfolds in the organization. As Stevenson and Weiner (2020) pointed out, "A plan doesn't govern people's day-to-day work; routines do." Therefore, a plan for CI, or diagrams and templates charting CI, will not govern educators' work. Instead, leaders should develop and promote routines so that educators' daily work is colored by CI. Coaches are likely involved in several organizational routines, such as data teams, instructional rounds, and communities of practice. Indeed, coaching itself is an organizational routine. No matter how many organizational routines individual coaches are a part of, we encourage thinking about how the routines of coaching not only implement the strategy but also improve that strategy. Next, we share examples of the enactment of CI across different levels, and each example illustrates differences in how districts embed coaching into CI routines.

(1) The instructional coaches at a turnaround elementary school are required to collect and report data and information such as the number of teachers they work with, the agendas for grade-level team meetings, and the notes from data team meetings. The information may be used by the coaches and the teachers, but even though it is given to building leaders, they collect it only to ensure that coaches and teachers are doing what they are supposed to, as part of the school's turnaround plan.

(2) The math coaches are supervised by the district math coordinator, who is himself an experienced coach. He meets with the coaches regularly and coaches the coaches. The chief academic officer was also a coach, and she coaches all the coordinators.

(3) The district literacy director, who is based at central office, meets with the school-based literacy coaches monthly. During the monthly meetings, they compare notes about what is going on across their different buildings, and the literacy director usually runs a protocol for what they have learned in the last month. He does not observe them coaching, because they are supervised by the principals. The assistant superintendent, who supervises the literacy director, never asks him about the coaches.

(4) The district hires retired principals as coaches for new principals, although they've never received any coaching training. The

coaches, because they work across many schools, learn a great deal about what is going on across the district, including struggles that new principals are facing. The assistant superintendent for talent management is supposed to meet with the coaches quarterly, but almost always cancels the meetings because she is pulled away to deal with more pressing concerns. As a result, no one interacts with the coaches to gain a sense of what they have learned about new principals.

Across these four vignettes, coaches garned copious information about educators and the reform context, but there are overlooked possibilities for linking insights and supporting improvement. The first scenario unfolds quite often; with coaching valued mostly for the part it plays in a plan. That is, the most important feature of the coaching becomes that it happens as stipulated by the plan. Coaches and administrators are frequently aware that this is the case, but in a setting where compliance with the plan matters and time is limited, coaches and leaders may believe they do not have other options.

In the second scenario, the math coordinator is supporting individual coaches in relatively robust ways. But this work is done coach by coach, and they do not have a mechanism for collecting data across the coaches to determine how coaching is influencing different outcomes. This coach-by-coach method is not uncommon in supervising coaching, yet it hinders efforts to improve coaching in a systemic manner.

In the third and fourth scenarios, coaching is seen as a support for teachers and leaders disconnected from other improvement work in the district. In the third scenario, there is variation in practice from school to school in terms of teaching and coaching, with system leaders neglecting to consider how to leverage coaching to close gaps in practice among schools. Here, we reiterate that, for coaching to matter, system leaders should braid coaching with strategy to further improvement across schools.

Finally, in the leadership coaching scenario, no one knows the quality of the coaching that is being provided to new principals. Regardless, these leadership coaches have insights into the workings of the district in addition to the strengths and challenges of new principals. Thus, there is a missed opportunity to listen to leadership coaches to determine necessary changes in systems, routines, and conditions enabling new principals to carry out their best work.

We now turn to a better-case scenario, in which coaches are part of several interlocking cycles of improvement. In Violet District, district administrators hired coaches to support a specific literacy program in the middle grades. As you might expect with a comprehensive literacy program, there was a lot for teachers to learn. The coaches worked with every literacy teacher every week, and they collected data about the rollout of the program, including what aspects of instruction were or were not being implemented. They did this not to monitor compliance or hold teachers accountable, but to inform plans for professional development. Specifically, they used data to make good use of time set aside for support of teachers. This helped ensure time was spent on aspects of the program where teachers needed the most help. To do so, the principal met with the coaches every week to learn about what they were seeing in classrooms, what the teachers were saying about what they needed, and to plan the next level of support. Notably, there were transparent, trustful conversations among coaches and principals about literacy reform efforts. At the same time, the coaches and the principal also analyzed what coaches needed to better support teachers, by surfacing questions and requests that the coaches did not feel equipped to respond to, and by using the data from the teachers about what they needed from the coaches.

CONTINUALLY IMPROVING COACHING

We have depicted how coaches play roles in continuous improvement, and now we turn the tables, asking: What happens if leaders apply the techniques of continuous improvement on coaching itself? That is, how can evidence be collected and analyzed to learn how to improve coaches' work to improve organizational outcomes? We articulate that what you measure depends on what you want to know, so sometimes, you are looking back on something to see whether or not it was successful. This is a summative approach in which you are doing an autopsy. Other times educators use a formative approach; they are looking forward to see how to improve something, which is similar to a physical. For coaching, a program evaluation, or summative assessment, is difficult, because many factors affect the outcomes of coaching.

For example, in the case of the literacy program, the ultimate goal of the coaching is to improve the literacy skills of the students. If students do benefit, it is very unlikely that coaching should take all the credit—the coaches do not teach the students directly, after all. The teachers also have something to do with it, not to mention the building and central office leaders, the board that approved the funding, and so on. In other words, the coaching *contributes* to the outcome, but the outcome cannot be directly *attributed* to the coaching. By the same token, if the literacy skills of students do not improve after instituting coaching, is coaching to blame? Perhaps coaching has not caused the expected change in teacher practice, yet there could be several reasons for that. Perhaps coaching has been in place for only a short period of time. Perhaps student skills even decreased—the implementation dip is the name given to the phenomenon whereby the intended outcomes contract while everyone learns the ins and outs of a new initiative.

For an instrument as multifaceted and embedded as coaching, a program evaluation that attempts to connect coaching to the intended outcomes is an involved and expensive undertaking. But that doesn't mean that we should give up on the idea of evaluating coaching, or settle for asking the clients whether they like their coach or find coaching useful. Indeed, from a CI perspective, it is necessary to continually check how coaching is working toward key outcomes. This involves using formative approaches while measuring the influences and impacts of coaching. That is, if leaders design coaching as a lever to advance their strategy, they need to know whether coaching is being enacted the way that they envisioned, so that they can use that information for two major purposes: to tinker with the coaching model to make it more effective, and to determine what support coaches need to better implement the coaching model. That support could be in the form of additional knowledge and skills, leadership actions, or other resources.

We caution that, in the same way that a summative assessment may come too late to help a student improve their understanding of the laws of motion or how to write a conclusion, a program evaluation may come too late to improve coaching as a support for a strategy. Also, just as a grade may tell a student how good something is without providing information about how to improve, a summative evaluation may provide information about how effective coaching is without providing information about how to make it better.

Knowing whether coaching is happening as proposed is important, but the interactions constituting coaching tend to be a "black box." In other words, while there are many models for coaching that describe what *ought* to be happening during coaching, often there is much less information about what is *actually* happening during coaching. Here, we care about how to measure coaching so that it can be improved, and, to do so, we need to understand what is happening during coaching; we need to get inside the black box. These efforts can provide information about how coaching is being enacted in a district and be useful to design capacity-building opportunities for educators in a particular context.

We share a few possibilities for gathering rich data on the implementation of coaching. The simplest way to know what coaching looks like is to observe coaches carrying out their daily work. The observer should not evaluate the client, and they should emphasize that they are there to observe the coaching and have no interest in the topic being discussed. Another option is to record coaches' work. This may seem awkward, but since everyone now carries a smartphone, having the app running during the coaching conversation is completely unobtrusive. This method has multiple benefits, including:

- The coach can listen to and reflect on their own coaching.
- Coaching conversations—or excerpts thereof—can be replayed for the purposes of professional learning of multiple coaches.
- The conversation can be transcribed for closer analysis. High-quality transcription is expensive, but there are low-cost and no-cost options that may be perfectly adequate for the purpose at hand.

If complete confidentiality is important, then the coach can be given in-
structions for getting the coaching conversation transcribed, scrubbing the
transcription of identifying features like the use of names, and uploading
the transcription anonymously to an online folder.

In place of, or in addition to, recording coaching, coaches and clients
can respond to a survey about the coaching experience. For this, it is beneficial to pair up the responses of coach and client, and that can be done by
asking the pair to assign themselves a name that makes them identifiable as
a pair—a superhero, sports team, or flower—but preserves their anonymity.

COACH EVALUATION

We just explored how system leaders can track successes and limitations of
coaching as a step in continuously improving coaching. But district leaders also seek to measure and monitor the strengths and weaknesses of
coaches. We are frequently asked about how district and/or school leaders
can evaluate coaches. Certainly, if districts are interested in using data to
improve the quality of coaching, then that is a plus. The following conversation associated with coach evaluation really happened, and we encourage paying attention to the concerns and priorities of the district leader:

Assistant Superintendent: We are looking to find someone to help us
   develop a tool for evaluating our instructional coaches—you
   know, something that mirrors our teacher evaluation instrument.
   I heard that you work with districts on coaching. Do you do this
   sort of thing?

Us: Great, thanks for reaching out. We are so happy that you are
   looking for ways to improve coaching. We need to know a bit
   more about what you have in mind. Can you start off by telling
   us what you're looking to accomplish?

Assistant Superintendent: Well, I guess we want to be able to hold
   coaches accountable.

Us: Can you tell us more about what you mean by that?

Assistant Superintendent: We want to make sure that people are doing
   what they are supposed to be doing. Obviously, the people we
   hired as coaches were chosen not just because they were great
   teachers, but also because they have really good people skills
   and are really reliable and hardworking. But there's a fairness
   issue; they are still part of the same bargaining unit as the rest of
   the teachers, and we don't want to be accused of treating them
   differently. And we need a paper trail if there ever was a problem
   with a coach, you know, whatever that would be.

Us: And is there any other aspect of evaluation that you are interested in?

Assistant Superintendent: Beyond holding coaches accountable?

Us: Yes.

Assistant Superintendent: Like what?

With regard to the assistant superintendent's quote, they were eager to have a conversation about different ways evaluation could be used to improve the skills of individual coaches, as well as to improve the quality of coaching overall. Through this, we teamed up to think through how CI could apply to coaching in this district. This included co-designing approaches for collecting and using multiple forms of data to take a pulse on the implementation of coaching. Table 7.1 offers examples of evidence to collect to continuously improve, or evaluate, coaching.

With awareness of the role of evaluation for compliance purposes, we underscore that CI is more focused on collecting data that will answer questions about progress toward a goal *so that* changes can be made to improve resulting outcomes. Many of the points from this chapter are not exclusive to coaching. In fact, we are strong proponents of examining all educational practices with an eye toward continuous improvement. This entails collecting and studying various forms of evidence and always striving to reach equity-oriented goals.

Table 7.1. Examples of how different sources of evidence can answer different questions about the effectiveness of coaching.

Major Question	Evidence to Collect and Analyze
Are coaches doing what they are supposed to be doing?	Coaching logs detailing which teachers they met with, on what dates, and for how long
Are coaches coaching well?	Observational data, either by sitting in on coaching sessions or by listening to recordings of coaching conversations
Are the coaches effective?	Survey data on teachers' perceptions about their experiences with coaching
	Observation data on teachers' instruction before and after coaching
	Student achievement data
Is coaching effective?	Analyze notes from classroom observations and patterns in student outcomes (e.g., test score results, student work samples)
	Survey data from principals on their perceptions about the ways coaches are influencing classroom practice and student outcomes

TO MAKE COACHING MATTER

This chapter drew on research, theory, and practice to make claims about the·interconnections of coaching and continuous improvement. We highlighted the role of district and school leaders in creating conditions for coaches to facilitate CI. Next, we list how district leaders, principals, and coaches can strengthen the infrastructure of coaching to support CI. These recommended leadership moves are associated with continuously improving coaching so that the system—in addition to coaches within the system—learn to improve.

District leaders should:

- assess organizational conditions for coaches and other leaders to engage in continuous improvement activities;
- evaluate how coaching contributes to strategic goals and priorities;
- analyze multiple forms of evidence on coaching to improve not only coaching, but also other aspects of the district/school;
- consider how multiple factors influence the effects of coaching on outcomes in and across schools; and
- develop coaches' capacity to engage in continuous improvement efforts.

Principals should:

- collect and analyze several forms of evidence on coaching in their building;
- discuss evidence on coaching with their coach and ask questions about how they can support the improvement of coaching; and
- include coaches in school-based continuous improvement processes.

Coaches should:

- participate in continuous improvement activities;
- collect, analyze, and reflect on multiple sources of data on their activities and outcomes; and
- develop teachers' understanding of facets of continuous improvement, including its links to strategy and equity.

This chapter advanced arguments about continuous improvement as a keystone for coaching. We illustrated how coaching reflects the tenets of CI, and, more concretely, how coaches engage in the practices of CI. This chapter, therefore, established how coaching—by its very design and definition—embraces learning to improve. It is evident that one constancy in coaching is a focus on learning, yet, as discussed in several sections of this book, there is wide variability in other structures, practices, and conceptualizations of coaching. Interrogating variations in coaching, Chapter 8 characterizes the spectrum of coaches operating in the education field. We point to affordances and limitations of various coaching models, targeting different elements of schooling. Further, the following chapter explores the infrastructure and leadership crucial to enable the implementation of diverse forms of coaching.

Permutations of Coaching

Let a hundred flowers bloom.

—Mao Zedong

When visualizing a coach, it is important to reflect and ask the following questions: What do you see? What do you hear? Who are they? What are they targeting? For many, their visions of coaching remain linked to the athletic and business fields; they may hear encouragements or questions. Across many districts and schools, people still imagine coaches blowing a whistle to gain attention or, more seriously, carrying a clipboard to jot notes or collect evidence within a teacher's classroom or while walking through the hallway with other leaders. Across systems, a coach may engage in many activities, target many issues, and operate within multiple models. Yet, one commonality—across visions of coaching and types of coaches— is that coaching supports improvement by bringing together a coach and client(s) for elbow-to-elbow work that promotes learning and improvement. The type of learning, or the target for improvement, in addition to the focus of this joint work, however, can have many permutations.

As levers for learning, equity, and change, coaching models cannot be treated as interchangeable. To optimize strategic, equitable coaching, we pull back the curtain on the array of coaching models present in the education sphere. While Chapter 2 explained how a coach, positioned in a single model, engages in multiple activities linked to adult learning and organizational improvement, this chapter illuminates features of multiple coaching models, discussing how system and school leaders adopt, implement, and navigate varied formulations of coaching. Thus, while pointing to commonalities in coaches' work, we portray the differences between them. Further, this chapter identifies areas of opportunity as well as potential hurdles when districts deploy multiple coaching models. Here, we argue that crafting coherence across coaching models and activities is vital. To translate this into practice, we explain how system leaders can unpack their full set of coaching models and clarify similarities and differences across models to benefit other leaders, teachers, and even coaches! In doing so, we remind reformers and administrators, as well as coaches and teachers, to clarify definitions of a particular coaching model, expectations on coaches' work in a particular model, and provide tailored support to coaches on their particular model.

NUMEROUS TYPES OF COACHES

In the book's introduction, we portrayed our experiences as, and ties to, a variety of coaches, from reading and equity coaches to leadership and running coaches. We have learned a great deal from multiple coaches addressing multiple facets of our professional and personal lives; these coaches were situated in different contexts, explicitly and implicitly leaning upon different coaching models. Moreover, we have observed and investigated how system leaders allocate funding and attention toward diverse coaching models employing multiple types of coaches in an attempt to improve several branches of teaching and leading. That is, we have seen leaders design and implement coaching models concentrating on everything from elementary mathematics instruction to high school ELA and from principal mentoring to turnaround reform. Depending on the model, coaches' work may extend beyond instructional improvement to address leadership, data analysis, behavior and attendance, family engagement, or other elements of schooling. Together, we have supported and/or studied over a dozen types of coaches, including:

- reading coaches;
- mathematics coaches;
- instructional coaches;
- other subject-specific coaches (e.g., science, social studies);
- English learner coaches;
- data coaches;
- new teacher coaches;
- new principal coaches;
- school improvement/turnaround coaches;
- equity coaches;
- technology coaches;
- classroom management coaches;
- family engagement coaches;
- leadership coaches; and
- district improvement coaches.

This list is not exhaustive, and you may be thinking of several other types of coaches! As portrayed in Figure 8.1, the spectrum of coaches is a testament to the popularity of coaching and to leaders' faith in coaching. This diversity of coaches indicates reformers and administrators rely on

Figure 8.1. A model of the spectrum of instructional, leadership, and reform coaches in the field of PK–12 schooling.

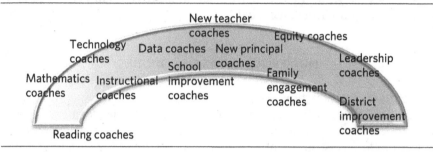

coaching as a tool to improve nearly any aspect of schooling. We also note that the diffusion of coaching into numerous educational arenas show how leaders applied—and adapted—ideas about coaching while striving to reach varied goals. For instance, we purport reformers in the coaching field applied tenets from new teacher coaching to design new principal coaching, and they applied tenets from instructional coaching to formulate technology coaching. It remains necessary to track the flow of ideas that guide the nature of these multiple types of coaching. In the following section, we dig into commonalities of, as well as key distinctions across, varieties of coaching. We argue tailored infrastructure and leadership are necessary to ensure each variety of coaching attains its potential.

SIMILARITIES AND DIFFERENCES ACROSS TYPES OF COACHES

Whether coaches are mathematics coaches, data coaches, or family engagement coaches, their position carries connotations regarding supporting change. Even more importantly, their work entails engaging in strategies to support learning and encourage both individual and organizational improvement. Extending points from Chapters 2 and 4, we highlight that each variety of coach should be working toward strategic, equitable change. But there exist key differences between the guiding conceptualizations and daily routines of mathematics and family engagement coaches, or across other varieties of coaches. Next, we illuminate important overlaps and distinctions across the coaching spectrum.

Similarities Across the Coaching Spectrum

First, most coaches listed along our spectrum (see Figure 8.1) conduct activities in which they meet and collaborate with individuals and teams of educators addressing the coach's focal area. For instance, literacy coaches meet with teams of teachers to analyze ELA data and discuss ELA instructional strategies. And novice principal coaches meet regularly with their set of novice principals, asking about recent leadership activities and dilemmas and the principal's development goals. Second, most coaches are intermediaries, sharing ideas and evidence with leaders at higher levels of their educational organization in addition to regular communication and engagement with their coachees. For example, literacy coaches often meet with district and school leaders to deliver updates on teachers' engagement with and responses to the reading curriculum. Further, these coaches may offer information to administrators on how they are targeting particular grade levels or domains of literacy in their coaching. Similarly, technology coaches garner information on schools' technology use and challenges, and they provide updates to central office administrators.

We underscore that, by collecting and communicating evidence, multiple varieties of coaching play a role in continuous improvement (see Chapter 7). Third, most types of coaches serve as a lighthouse—the strong, bright reminder of the importance of their issue, or for their specialty area. For example, the adoption of district mathematics coaches sends a clear message about the priority of math instructional improvement for the district, and the adoption of equity coaches beams a clear message about the priority of tackling inequities across the district.

Distinctions Across the Coaching Spectrum

Although they possess shared tenets, each "flavor" of coaching uses different routines and leans upon different structures and conceptions. For example, the routines of an effective data coach differ from those of an effective reading coach. This is because data coaches must devote substantial time to analyzing multiple forms of data and presenting data displays to different audiences. In comparison, the routines of a reading coach include spending a larger proportion of time in classrooms and in teacher PLC sessions to understand the nature of reading instruction and build teachers' capacity regarding the content and pedagogy of reading instruction (Coburn & Woulfin, 2012; Matsumura et al., 2010). Based upon this, district and school leaders should ask—and assess—how systems offer support for each type of coach. We have partnered with district leaders to map their array of coaches, listing what each variety focuses on as well as how district and school leaders support each variety. Next, we facilitated conversations on how district and school leaders could provide other learning opportunities to enable each type of coach to do their best work. Later in this chapter, we describe how to chart and improve supports for differing types of coaches within a single system.

Coaches who engage in varied forms of coaching draw on different sets of knowledge and skills. Returning to the contrast between data and reading coaches, these two types of coaches must apply different knowledge and skills. A data coach should have knowledge, skills, and competencies regarding collecting, analyzing, displaying, and communicating multiple forms of data (Marsh et al., 2010; Farrell, 2015). They should be able to produce charts and diagrams and also develop others' capacity to examine data to drive change. Turning to a contrasting example, a reading coach should have knowledge, skills, and competencies tied to multiple elements of reading instruction, the reading curriculum and assessments, and how students progress as readers (Bean, 2015; Coburn & Woulfin, 2012). More concretely, they should be able to explain and promote components of the adopted reading curriculum and assessments while also being able to develop teachers' understanding of the reading development trajectory across grade levels. Notably, an effective reading coach is not necessarily an effective data, equity, or leadership coach. As such, district and school leaders should hire, develop, and support coaches with an eye toward the focus and features of their specific variety. This involves administrators ensuring an appropriate match between who is hired into what coaching role.

HOW LEADERS BOLSTER VARIOUS TYPES OF COACHES

District and school leaders, in addition to coaches, should be cognizant of differences among the spectrum of coaches by asking questions, including:

- Which coaches are coaching which educators?
- What are the major goals of each type of coach?
- How are various types of coaches working toward the district strategy?
- How are various types of coaches working to promote equity?
- What are the core routines of each type of coach?
- How is each type of coach supported and supervised?

For example, which sets of educators are mathematics, behavior, and leadership coaches coaching? If new teachers are paired with mathematics and behavior coaches, they will need time to engage with each coach, and they may hear different ideas on how to set up their classroom environment and routines. In this case, it is crucial to provide common, clear guidance to support new teachers.

As another example, how are reading and science coaches in the same district advancing ideas about respective curricula while coaching teachers? If reading coaches recommend teachers allocate extensive time for small-group literacy instruction with "centers," this may clash with the science coach's requests related to launching a new model of science instruction. How will teachers make sense of competing ideas from their reading and science coaches? And are principals aware of key messages from the reading and science coaches on using instructional time and setting up the classroom environment? As another example, how are district-based versus school-based coaches engaging in equity-centered coaching? Here, we reiterate the importance that all coaches, whether those focused on reading, turnaround, or new principals, should engage in equity-centered coaching.

We offer insights on organizational supports and learning opportunities associated with emergent forms of coaching. To ground these discussions, we delve into technology, equity, and leadership coaching as examples. We have seen technology, equity, and leadership coaches operating in isolation or with limited guidance from central office. Consequently, these coaches may lack the tools to address adult learning and systemic improvement. More specifically, we have identified technology coaches who are proficient in the operational aspects of ordering devices and troubleshooting Internet issues. Yet, these coaches would benefit from PD on how to develop teachers' knowledge, skills, and dispositions for infusing technology into instruction.

Similarly, in some districts, equity coaches desire to conduct equity audits or analyze particular forms of evidence through an equity lens, yet they may not be provided with the time or may not have been properly introduced by principals to regularly engage in those routines with teachers (Blaisdell, 2018). And, for the final example of leadership coaching, we have observed intermediary organizations' leadership coaches conduct high-leverage coaching activities with principals. Yet, when the reform shifts, resulting in dropping the district's contract with the intermediary organization, principal coaching is discontinued, indicating sustainability challenges for this type of coaching from an intermediary organization.

We highlight that, across these examples, it is important for system leaders to attend to: who is coaching whom; how various forms of coaching will align with strategy; how each type of coach will be introduced and supported; and how each type of coaching will be continually improved so that it reaches its aim. When educational leaders discuss and document answers to these questions on their array of coaches, it can support the improvement of conditions for coaching, and, in turn, make coaching matter. Further, if leaders address these questions, they can develop infrastructure for each type of coach as well as increase clarity for teachers and school leaders on the underlying purpose of each type of coach. These leadership activities help construct positive working conditions for coaches while also raising clients' receptivity to coaching. In sum, these efforts set the stage for a strong coaching culture, raising the potential for coaching to meet strategic, equity-oriented goals.

FEATURES OF DIVERSE COACHING MODELS

Since we care about the conditions and leadership enabling multiple types of coaches to do their best work, not only for supporting individual learning but for promoting strategic improvement, we shed light on structural features of coaching models. Specifically, we describe three design features shaping coaches' activities and educators' responses: (1) where coaching is based, (2) how much power/authority coaches hold, and (3) how specialized the coaching is. Throughout, we encourage attention to the overlapping—yet diverse—needs of various coaching models. We remind reformers and leaders that each coaching model has features influencing its design, how educators perceive the model, coaches' daily work, and, ultimately, the quality and impact of the coaching itself.

The Homes of Coaching

Coaches can be positioned, or based, in various spots in the education system. This is due to coaching models being district based, school based, or even based in external reform organizations. Depending on where a coaching model is based, coaches hold different levels of power and authority, different degrees of access to coachees and their organizations, and have more or less information about coachees and their organizational realities. Therefore, the home of coaching influences coaches' work, including how they engage with other educators and how their work reflects strategic priorities from the organization.

We have seen district-based leadership coaches adopted to steer principals' work and deemed as enforcers of central office's strategic goals. These leadership coaches may possess the coach title, yet their targets are designed by other district leaders. Sometimes this entails the leadership coach taking up supervisory duties, such as conducting evaluations of the principal (Honig & Rainey, 2020). We have also seen school-based instructional coaches deployed to support all teachers in refining instruction. These coaches may be deemed as colleagues, with strong connections to teachers and the site but with zero formal authority to control routines or change practices. The low degree of authority may prevent coaches from optimally distributing their efforts and time toward teachers with particular instructional needs.

A coaching model's "home base" also matters as it determines who hires and supervises coaches. For example, if a principal both hires and closely supervises an instructional coach for their school, they are able to better ensure a fit between the coach and the building's culture. In contrast, an external reform organization coach may not supervise their data coaches in a manner aligned to the vision or approaches of the district or school. Moreover, the reform organization coach may not have insights as to the school's previous approaches to assessment, instruction, and collaboration (Trujillo & Woulfin, 2014). In this case, the distance also poses challenges for how often the coach engages with their coachees and the degree to which the coach is aware of contextual conditions shaping coachees' practices plus beliefs and dispositions.

The coach's home base is typically the source of PD and other supports for that set of coaches. That is, district- and school-based coaches encounter professional development facilitated by their system leaders, but reform organization coaches engage in PD offered by their direct leaders. In Chapter 6, we described approaches to developing and supporting coaches in different venues to optimize their work. Again, we encourage careful attention to the affordances as well as potential drawbacks of arms-reach, diffuse coaching from reform organizations.

Power to the Coaches

Depending on the coaching model, coaches hold different degrees of power. A coach's power matters for: (1) who they focus on and report to, and (2) how they support and monitor improvement (Mangin & Dunsmore, 2015). For example, a district leadership coach may coach principals while reporting to the superintendent or the district's leadership director. And a school-based literacy coach typically coaches teachers in an elementary school while reporting to the principal. In certain cases, school-based coaches, holding less power over teachers than administrators, function in a teacher leadership role (Wenner & Campbell, 2017).

A major allure of coaching is that coaches serve as informal leaders with deep awareness of people and their context, and they are able to form trusting relationships to work together toward change. We highlight that, as informal leaders, coaches are asked to build relationships and foster adult learning to motivate improvement (Aguilar, 2013).

With regard to leadership titles, coaches typically do not serve as administrators. With regard to leadership duties, coaches typically do not conduct formal evaluations and have limited managerial responsibilities (Tschannen-Moran & Tschannen-Moran, 2010). We raise the point, however, that, in some systems, coaches engage in tasks linked to evaluation and operations. Specifically, in some charter management organizations, coaches conduct teacher observations using formal evaluation tools (Galey-Horn & Woulfin, 2021). And in some districts, district-based principal supervisors conduct leadership coaching with a set of principals while holding responsibility for evaluating them. Once again, tracking and categorizing coaches' on-the-ground work is necessary to detect what level of power coaches can exercise within a context, as well as to consider how to create support to boost coaching.

Specialization of the Coaching Model

Coaching models vary by their level of specialization or the degree to which coaches target a particular reform, content area, or set of educational issues. At one extreme, some districts and schools use coaches, similar to the Reading First reading coach model, to develop K–3 teachers' knowledge and skills of reading instruction (Deussen et al., 2007; Kersten & Pardo, 2007). These coaches provide specialized PD on pillars of early reading instruction matching the adopted curriculum (Coburn & Woulfin, 2012). These coaches also use walkthrough forms to collect evidence on how teachers' instruction matches pillars of early reading instruction. In contrast, some districts rely on improvement coaches to advance the superintendent's plan or a set of initiatives (Woulfin, 2018). These coaches are tasked with leading change across content areas; this places an onus on coaches to understand a wide set of standards and programs. Oftentimes, improvement coaches engage with school leaders to ensure communication and activities match district priorities. If adopting this model, we encourage collaboration between improvement coaches and school leaders to determine focal areas so that a coach can concentrate their work with educators at a particular moment.

There are benefits and drawbacks to a highly specialized coaching model. A coach's specialty may be relevant to some educators in a school or district, but not all. For example, a district-based science coach may collaborate with teams of middle school science teachers and high school science departments while rarely engaging with those schools' English teachers or principals. In turn, some educators may receive focused, tailored support on science, while other educators experience limited touchpoints with the science coach. A coaching model's inclusivity, or span, influences teachers' and leaders' beliefs and dispositions about coaching. In particular, if educators are required to work with several types of coaches, they may begin to see coaching as a burden. In contrast, if a coach neglects working with them, educators may see the coach as exclusionary. To optimize the coaching model, system and school leaders should clearly present who is coaching whom for what purpose. Thus, leaders should answer the question: How will coaches work toward strategic, equitable change by focusing on certain educators in certain contexts?

Although we have heard educators mention being over-coached in a few contexts, we more commonly hear educators describe being under-coached. In these cases, teachers disappointedly report:

> Well, I met the coach last year, and she did a couple walkthroughs during the winter, and we tried scheduling a debrief conversation, but it got canceled. And then we found a time to discuss math centers, but now I think it would be great to see her model small group math instruction. . . . [I] am not sure how to find a time for that.

Here, the teacher is frustrated with challenges of connecting with their coach, and they would appreciate an opportunity to engage with the coach again to close the loop and foster learning. Simultaneously, many coaches mention feeling swamped or spread too thin, with not enough time to meet the needs of each coachee. We've heard, for instance, leadership coaches admitting:

> I schedule site visits every 2–3 weeks with my principals, but sometimes the schedule shifts, so there's lots of emailing and texting to trouble-shoot challenges and prep for planning meetings. I wish I had days in the school for that side-by-side work with principals, especially those newer principals.

These vignettes showcase barriers faced by coaches as well as coachees to fully enact coaching routines on a regular basis. To help counter these barriers, we encourage leaders to be attuned to how models include various educators and provide clarity on how and why coaches will engage with specific educators to work toward reaching strategic goals. This transparency on the how and why of coaching models assists so educators feel neither ignored (under-coached) nor under the microscope (over-coached) and so that, ultimately, coaching is optimized. Again, we encourage system and campus leaders to instruct others about the definitions and purposes of multiple coaching models. At the same time, we acknowledge that multiple, coexisting coaching models can enable *or* hinder learning and improvement efforts. In light of this, the following section devotes attention to how leaders can more effectively harness the power and potential of coaching by analyzing and aligning varieties of coaching in their context.

ORGANIZING A BLIZZARD OF COACHING

We applaud the energy for improving multiple facets of schooling and the enthusiasm for coaching, but is this blizzard of coaching and coaches feasible and sustainable? There are steep costs to enacting coaching initiatives (Knight, 2012). Midsized districts with about 30 schools may spend *over $5 million annually* on coaching for various educators and staff. And leaders and teachers can become overburdened and confused rather than supported, as a result of engaging with multiple types of coaches. As described earlier in this chapter, multiple coaches may carry inconsistent or burdensome messages to educators. Additionally, different types of coaches may adopt different coaching practices (i.e., team-based coaching, curriculum-focused coaching, co-teaching, cognitive coaching) that take time for others to learn about, participate in, and respond to (Aguilar, 2013; Farrell, 2015; Gibbons & Cobb, 2016; Matsumura et al., 2010).

Across several states and districts, we have seen teachers work with several types of coaches who use different coaching techniques. For instance, some elementary teachers engage with literacy, math, and reform coaches as part of school improvement efforts. Literacy coaches may elect to concentrate their work in grade-level team meetings, math coaches may focus on in-classroom coaching cycles, and reform coaches may focus on PD with leadership team walkthroughs. A teacher may engage with these three coaches in vastly different ways. And the teacher may juggle different routines and negotiate different norms with the three coaches. Moreover, these three types of coaches may tell a single teacher to change classroom practice in three opposing ways! This raises several questions: How should teachers make sense of conflicting messages from coaches? How can the messaging, and/or activities, from multiple coaches reinforce key messages to support educator learning? It is evident coaches' messaging can harmonize or clash, so leaders, reformers, and researchers must pay greater attention to the influences of multiple coaches on educators and improvement efforts.

The widespread application of coaching signals that educational organizations, and their leaders and educators, desire improvement. We are keenly aware of the need for improving multiple components of teaching, learning, and schooling, but we wonder whether the spread of coaching indicates, in actuality, that leaders are currently trying to "fix" too much at once. Considering this issue, we turn attention to the importance of leaders aligning and continually improving their multiple coaching models so that each type of coach can work strategically. As discussed in Chapter 7, continuous improvement of coaching is vital to ensure coaching works to advance strategic priorities and assists in reaching equity-oriented objectives. Finally, coaching should never become part of the too-muchness of educational reform and school improvement. As such, leaders must streamline coaching models and check the conditions for coaching.

In light of the proliferation of coaching, it is vital for district and school leaders to track multiple (and sometimes competing!) coaching models in their system. They should map the various types of coaches, what each type of coach is targeting, and who each type of coach focuses on; see Table 8.1. By mapping coaching models, leaders can view who is coaching in what ways on what topics and under what conditions. For example, this mapping could show that both reading and equity coaches are facilitating PLCs on culturally responsive instruction, so it is necessary to consider how coaches can reinforce common messages to promote aligned change. It may also show that leadership and reform organization coaches are engaging with principals on how to collect classroom observation data in distinctly different ways; this could result in confusion. In light of this, it becomes important to ensure the messages on what and how to improve build upon each other to foster learning, as opposed to clashing and confusing coachees.

Table 8.1. A sample coaching map from a midsized district.

Type of Coach	Purpose of the Coaching	Which Schools and/or Educators They'll Target	Who Develops and Supports These Coaches
Elementary literacy coaches	Improve ELA instruction and outcomes	K–3 teachers	Director of ELA
Elementary mathematics coaches	Improve mathematics instruction and outcomes	K–5 teachers	Director of mathematics
Secondary literacy coaches	Improve ELA instruction and outcomes in middle/high schools	6–12 ELA teachers	Director of ELA
Secondary mathematics coaches	Improve mathematics instruction and outcomes in middle/high schools	6–12 mathematics teachers	Director of mathematics
District data coaches	Promote data use across K–12 schools	Principals; 3–12 teachers	Chief academic officer
District equity coaches	Advance equity initiatives across K–12 schools	Principals; K–12 teachers	Director of equity and inclusion

Finally, just as coaches prioritize strategic areas of improvement, district and school leaders should set—and communicate—priorities associated with types of coaching. For example, a district may elect to concentrate time and PD on district improvement coaching and equity coaching during a 2-year period, with the plan to shift attention toward math coaching during the subsequent year. In this way, leaders would draft a strategic, extended plan for coaching. Further, leaders would clearly communicate this plan on coaching, as an instrument, to teachers and other leaders to prevent surprises or misunderstandings on the nature of multiple coaching models. This could also reduce competition among coaching models. Of course, coaches would also be informed of the centrality of their work at different times, in different places, and on different topics. These plans, as well as the role clarity for coaches, would help make coaching matter.

TO MAKE COACHING MATTER

In this chapter, we shone light on the spectrum of coaching, noting important similarities and differences across varieties of coaching. We described benefits and challenges of instituting multiple coaching models within a district or school. Here, we acknowledged that coaching is multifaceted and oftentimes loosely defined, coaches wear many hats, and districts and schools have adopted multiple models of coaching. Addressing these conditions, the following lists provide recommendations for how district leaders, principals, and coaches can make sense of—and foster coherence across—permutations of coaching. In particular, we encourage both district and school leaders to analyze the structures and practices of each type of coach in their system and clearly frame the purposes of coaching to other educators. Additionally, we invite district and school leaders to unite different types of coaches for collaborative learning opportunities that support the implementation of strategic, equity-centered coaching. And we underscore that coherence across coaching holds an important role so that educators perceive and experience coaching as a support for learning and improvement, as opposed to a burden linked to accountability.

District leaders should:

- map all types of coaches in their district;
- clearly define and communicate roles and responsibilities for each type of coach;
- provide tailored professional learning opportunities for each type of coach;
- provide opportunities for different types of coaches to meet, collaborate, and discuss their work; and
- collect evidence on the nature of different types of coaching and check for coherence across types.

Principals should:

- understand the focus and routines of each type of coach working in their school;
- gain a sense of who each coach will work with and assess whether coaches will overburden any teacher(s);
- clearly explain the purpose of each type of coach working in their school; and
- create and maintain structures and routines enabling each type of coach to conduct their core work.

Coaches should:

- understand the variety of other coaches also working in their context;
- clearly explain to coachees the focus, purpose, and format of their particular type of coaching; and
- collect evidence from coachees on the potential overlap and burdens of multiple types of coaching.

Conclusion

Our author team has reflected on coaching while serving as coaches, while coaching coaches, and while studying coaches. And, because of the promise and potential of coaching and the assets of stellar coaches we have known and worked with, we repeatedly loop back to the question: How can we make coaching matter even more than it currently does? That is, how can reformers and leaders take coaching, an instrument that is central to improving teaching and leading, and give it more power to do better? How can reformers and leaders create conditions that sustain coaching, enable coaches to do their best work, and foster deep change to reach critical goals?

Responding to these multidimensional questions, this book has illuminated and illustrated how system and school leaders can optimize coaching, improve coaches' working conditions, raise the quality of coaching, and enable strategic, equitable change efforts. We showcased the past, present, and future of coaching, including acknowledging its ties to waves of accountability policy and depicting its counter normative approach. As such, we shone light on how coaching disrupts facets of schooling; coaching literally opens classroom and school doors, and it opens windows for adult learning. Coaches' presence propels changes in how teachers and leaders "do school."

In addition, we portrayed how the design and structures of coaching models as well as the supports for implementing coaching can be bolstered so that coaches can work toward strategic, equity-centered goals. In turn, we presented the nature of coaches' work within a refined coaching system. This includes unpacking coaches' role in equity audits (Chapter 4) and continuous improvement routines (Chapter 7). We also described how principals and teachers would benefit from professional learning opportunities (Chapter 6) so that they develop a deep understanding of how and why to engage in coaching. Therefore, we care about the learning necessary for deeply implementing coaching to promote meaningful change across the education system.

STRIDES TO IMPROVE SCHOOLING AND COACHING

Because our education system needs improvement and dismantling of racist and ableist approaches to teaching and leading, this book explicitly revolves around strategic, equity-centered coaching. Our starting point is that all coaching aligns to strategic goals; all coaching serves to reach equity-oriented goals. Coaching cannot leave behind children, communities, or educators, nor can coaching function in the absence of a vision for improvement. Based upon these guiding principles, coaching models must center equity, and coaches must center equity in all aspects of their work. Whether engaging with teachers or principals and whether focused on literacy or science instruction or leadership, coaches should be raising points about how Black and Brown students and how students with disabilities are faring. In this manner, coaching smashes the siloes of equity and instructional improvement.

Additionally, school and district leaders should be clear about the connections between coaching and strategy. Leaders' communication and documentation on strategic coaching do not need to be long or elaborate; indeed, a simple T-chart listing strategic priorities and what coaches will do, or a diagram of priorities with an arrow noting how coaches will address it during elbow-to-elbow work with coachees, may be sufficient to spark discussion and promote strategy-aligned coaching. We continually remind leaders that 90 minutes, one piece of poster-paper, and three colored markers should be sufficient for crafting a strategic plan. Keeping the plan—for systemic improvement and strategic coaching—simple helps administrators and coaches translate ideas on paper (or from a PowerPoint) into action.

We are not the first to write about coaching, but we believe we are the first to tackle how infrastructure and leadership shape coaching, as well as to offer insights on how to refine structures and practices to improve coaching to promote strategic, equitable improvement. Importantly, we do not have all the answers, and we cannot present the "best" way to arrange coaching or the "best" way to support coaches. Instead, we invite leaders, educators, reformers, and policymakers—plus researchers—to listen to each other, learn together, and find ways to coach each other to help make coaching matter in various contexts. This means taking the time to ask what is working and what is challenging about coaching. And it means developing tailored solutions to build capacity on coaching and motivate others to engage in coaching. This reflects multiple points on continuous improvement from Chapter 7. And we'll return to this notion of partnering with researchers to foster strategic, equitable improvement. However, simply stated: Keep trying to define and refine coaching, keep doing the work of coaching, and keep growing as leaders, as coaches, as educational organizations. For coaching to make a difference, coaches should engage in core coaching activities for multiple days and weeks, and leaders must create positive conditions for coaching to unfold hour by hour and minute by minute. These conditions are much more than funding and time; they include the ecosystem for ongoing individual and organizational learning.

In multiple chapters, we tagged problematic elements of coaching systems and, on occasion, coaches' work. Here, we pronounce that, although we dissected coaching models, described gaps in leadership for coaching, and pointed to concerning patterns in coaches' work, we never aim to critique educators nor their ground-level conditions. Instead, we propose a new path in which the infrastructure for strategic, equity-centered coaching is fortified and aligned (Woulfin & Gabriel, 2020). Relying on leadership and capacity building, this approach involves making continuous improvements to coaching and the conditions for coaching. This means looking closely at what is working and what sticking points prevent coaches from engaging in high-leverage activities. Applying a continuous improvement stance toward coaching signals that coaching is a priority and, perhaps more importantly, that even coaches need to grow. Our supportive approach helps sustain coaching models while helping coaches reach vital system- and school-level goals; this is what makes coaching matter.

THEORIES IN AND FOR COACHING

This book addressed questions on how to refine and support coaching across multiple levels of the education system. As shown in Figure 1.1 from the Introduction, we make sense of coaching as stretching across analytic levels. At the macro-level, coaching is an instrument for driving educational reform. At the meso-level, coaching represents an organizational role that can promote collaboration and change. And, at the micro-level, coaching is a conversation, a set of interactions with sensemaking as people share, listen, and learn. Yet, we underscore the blurriness of these levels, including the ways coaching dynamics are influenced by factors at different levels. For instance, one-on-one coaching conversations about reading comprehension instruction are shaped in important ways by the school's organizational conditions as well as by the policy messages on reading instruction. Moreover, district and school leaders can set the stage, making a difference in how coaching is defined and how coaches are introduced; this, in turn, colors the nature of coaches' micro-work with educators.

Drawing on theories of organizations and adult learning, we portrayed how coaching influences the dynamics of change efforts. Notably, we first described how structures, policies, and resources steer coaching and the format of coaches' work. Next, we explicated how organizational conditions enable coaches' work. Finally, we provided insights on how coaching fosters adult learning through feedback and reflective conversations explicitly linked to equity and social justice. We encourage applying conceptual lenses to understand the nature of and improve coaching (Woulfin & Allen, 2022). And, as described in Chapter 6, we also encourage leaders and educator preparation program instructors to grapple with these theories in learning experiences for current and aspiring coaches, principals, and system leaders. We deem these theories as potent tools for analyzing evidence, examining issues, and solving problems.

As part of linking theory to practice to make coaching matter, we elevated how research can support improvement. First, there remains a need for multiple forms of research on coaching policies, models, and routines. For example, scholars should collect and analyze data on design features of coaching models as well as organizational conditions to answer questions about the ways the design of coaching shapes practice in schools. These studies could uncover insights on how many principals leadership coaches should coach, or how collaboration time is carved out for coaching activities. Second, scholars should devote attention to the work routines of leadership coaches and equity coaches to surface information on these varieties of coaching. For example, how do equity coaches engage in questioning and providing feedback? And what are the conditions enabling equity coaches to accelerate substantive changes in practice?

Opportunities also exist for policymakers, reformers, advocates, and educational administrators to draw on research to guide decision-making about coaching, professional learning, equity-oriented reforms, and strategic planning. At times, theoretical pieces or pieces from fields external to education (e.g., literature from the nonprofit sector or health-care field) could support efforts to refine coaching (Woulfin & Allen, 2022). Finally, we encourage meaningful partnerships between researchers and practitioners to co-design tools and supports for coaching (Coburn & Penuel, 2016). This could look like researchers partnering with district leaders to deeply understand—and improve—the coaching model. In addition, researchers can collect and analyze evidence on coaches' professional learning opportunities, including their perceptions of PD and the benefits of leader preparation coursework.

COACHING IN THE COVID-19 ERA

While drafting the initial outline for this book in 2019, we leaned on professional and personal experiences from the 1990s, 2000s, and 2010s. We reflected on districts and schools where coaching was embraced and where coaches leapt into action as well as sites where coaches operated under vague directions or struggled to partner with administrators. We synthesized empirical and conceptual literature on coaching, professional development, and organizational change, and noodled on future directions for coaching policy and coaches' work. Neither a global pandemic nor a rapid pivot to remote learning were typed into that outline! However, as we complete this manuscript in 2022, it is vital to attend to the intersection of coaching and pandemic schooling.

First, the U.S. education system cannot and should not return to "normal." In fact, we are wholly in favor of throwing normalcy out the window! We desire, as Ladson-Billings (2021) declared, re-setting the education system; coaches should be involved in this re-set. More concretely, coaches can re-set how educators learn, look at evidence, discuss equity challenges, and collaborate to ensure each child experiences responsive, engaging learning opportunities every day. We highlight that this means that coaching itself must be re-set to function as an instrument for strategic, equitable improvement.

Second, pandemic schooling pulled back the curtain on the heavy load schools, teachers, and educational leaders are expected to carry for society (Bartlett, 2022; Cotto & Woulfin, 2021; Pressley et al., 2021). This means coaches, too, are overburdened and may experience burnout. As such, reducing the too-muchness of coaching is crucial. We propose that district and school leaders should streamline coaches' responsibilities so that coaches can conduct their core work related to promoting adult and organizational learning. These leaders should be cognizant of the logistical tasks and administrative burdens placed on coaches (Herd & Moynihan, 2019), including the paperwork associated with coaching routines. Here, we emphasize that coaches do *not* need to complete forms on each step of the coaching cycle.

Third, the shocks of COVID-19 and pivots to remote learning disrupted the instructional opportunities of millions of children. The current evidence on "COVID slide" shows that inequities widened as a result of the pandemic (Goldhaber et al., 2022). Consequently, we argue coaching models must prioritize equity and coaches must attend to inequities in classrooms, schools, and districts. The shocks of the pandemic also disrupted professional learning opportunities for millions of teachers, leaders, staff, and aspiring educators. When school buildings closed, professional development was transposed to the online format, and many coaches shifted to virtual coaching, including observing online instruction and providing feedback in the Zoom chat box (Ippolito et al., 2021). It is likely educators' informal learning was dinged to an even greater extent. That is, teachers and leaders missed opportunities to discuss unit plans, instructional methods, and student progress in their school building's lunch room, hallway, and school parking lot; they could not ask questions or share ideas while waiting in the copy room (Woulfin & Allen, 2022). Of course, many coaches and leaders used a range of devices, apps, and strategies to communicate and learn together, even while socially distancing for health and safety. We note, however, that, as teachers and leaders readjust to in-person schooling and to pandemic-associated challenges, coaches play a crucial role in reconnecting individuals, fostering interactions in a caring manner, with an eye toward individual and collective learning.

Fourth, the stresses of the pandemic, combined with pre-existing pressures on schools and educators, leads us to discuss the elephant in the room: educator retention. There has been much discourse regarding a potential exodus of teachers and leaders who are sick and tired of unsatisfactory working conditions, mounting accountability and political pressures, and low pay (Lopez, 2022). While we are uncertain of the specific numbers of teachers, coaches (oy vey!), principals, superintendents, paraprofessionals, bus drivers, food service workers, and other staff who will depart the education field (Barnum, 2022; El-Bawab, 2022), we remain concerned because people shape the culture of districts and schools, and profoundly influence the quality of every aspect of students' educational experience. Here, we pronounce that robust, aligned coaching systems hold much potential for improving working conditions for teachers and leaders. Coaching can elevate care while encouraging improvement. That is, coaches can deliver targeted support to educators facing challenges and/or considering departing the education field. Further, coaches can support novice educators in a context, functioning as a bridge between educator preparation programs and schools. In these ways, coaches play an integral role in the path to recovery for the education system, schools, educators, students, and families.

SIGNED, SEALED, DELIVERED

Our author team adores letters (i.e., fabulous letters from Sarah's French grandmother, Isobel's longstanding *Coaching Letter*, a 2nd-grade writing standard!) nearly as much as we adore coaching, so we close with a letter to coaches:

Dear Coaches,

Thank you for supporting improvement in our schools and communities. Your work matters!

Thank you for noticing what is working and what is broken. Thank you for encouraging improvement and making us think hard about what is just and what needs to change. Thank you for boosting us up as you encourage us to grow. Thank you for lighting the way—even on challenging days and weeks.

Your power is that you remind us why we work in schools, what we want schools to be like, and how we want every child to experience exemplary learning opportunities every day. You are courageous because you use your heart to make a difference for educators, children, and communities. We see your courage when you lead for equity and when you lead toward the strategic plan.

We are grateful for all that we have learned about coaching; we look forward to learning even more from coaches and other leaders. We are hopeful *Making Coaching Matter* supports you in some way, and we are always here to listen to ideas and questions.

Warmly,
Sarah, Isobel, & Kerry

References

Aguilar, E. (2013). *The art of coaching: Effective strategies for school transformation*. John Wiley & Sons.

Aguilar, E. (2016). *The art of coaching teams: Building resilient communities that transform schools*. John Wiley & Sons.

Aguilar, E. (2020). *Coaching for equity: Conversations that change practice*. John Wiley & Sons.

Aguilar, E., Goldwasser, D., & Tank-Crestetto, K. (2011). Support principals, transform schools. *Educational Leadership, 69*(2).

Anagnostopoulos, D. (2003). The new accountability, student failure, and teachers' work in urban high schools. *Educational Policy, 17*(3), 291–316.

Annamma, S. A., Jackson, D. D., & Morrison, D. (2017). Conceptualizing color-evasiveness: Using dis/ability critical race theory to expand a color-blind racial ideology in education and society. *Race Ethnicity and Education, 20*(2), 147–162.

Argyris, C. (1990). *Overcoming organizational defenses: Facilitating organizational learning*. Allyn and Bacon.

Baker, B. D. (2021). *Educational inequality and school finance: Why money matters for America's students*. Harvard Education Press.

Bandura, A. (1977). Self-efficacy: Toward a unifying theory of behavioral change. *Psychological Review, 84*(2), 191.

Barnum, M. (2022). Uptick but no exodus. Retrieved May 14, 2022, from https://www.chalkbeat .org/2022/3/9/22967759/teacher-turnover-retention-pandemic-data

Bartlett, L. (2022). Specifying hybrid models of teachers' work during COVID-19. *Educational Researcher*, https://doi.org/0013189X211069399

Bean, R. M. (2015). *The reading specialist: Leadership and coaching for the classroom, school, and community*. Guilford Publications.

Bean, R. M., Draper, J. A., Hall, V., Vandermolen, J., & Zigmond, N. (2010). Coaches and coaching in Reading First schools: A reality check. *The Elementary School Journal, 111*(1), 87–114.

Bickman, L., Goldring, E., De Andrade, A. R., Breda, C., & Goff, P. (2012). Improving principal leadership through feedback and coaching. *Society for Research on Educational Effectiveness*.

Billingsley, B., & Bettini, E. (2019). Special education teacher attrition and retention: A review of the literature. *Review of Educational Research, 89*(5), 697–744.

Blaisdell, B. (2018). Beyond discomfort? Equity coaching to disrupt whiteness. *Whiteness and Education, 3*(2), 162–181.

Blase J., & Blase, J. (2003). *Handbook of instructional leadership: How successful principals promote teaching and learning*. Corwin Press.

Bocala, C., & Boudett, K. P. (2022). Looking at data through an equity lens. Retrieved May 1, 2022, from https://www.ascd.org/el/articles/looking-at-data-through-an-equity-lens

Boudett, K. P., City, E. A., & Murnane, R. J. (Eds.). (2020). *Data wise, revised and expanded edition: A step-by-step guide to using assessment results to improve teaching and learning*. Harvard Education Press.

Bristol, T. J. (2020). A tale of two types of schools: An exploration of how school working conditions influence black male teacher turnover. *Teachers College Record, 122*(3), 1–41.

Bryk, A. S., Gomez, L. M., Grunow, A., & LeMahieu, P. G. (2015). *Learning to improve: How America's schools can get better at getting better*. Harvard Education Press.

Bryk, A. S., & Schneider, B. (2002). *Trust in schools: A core resource for improvement*. Russell Sage Foundation.

Campbell, J., & van Nieuwerburgh, C. (2017). *The leader's guide to coaching in schools: Creating conditions for effective learning*. Corwin Press.

Center for Urban Education. (2015). Retrieved April 2, 2022, from https://cpb-us-e1.wpmucdn
   .com/sites.usc.edu/dist/6/735/files/2017/02/CUE-Protocol-Workbook-Final_Web.pdf

Coburn, C. E. (2001). Collective sensemaking about reading: How teachers mediate reading
   policy in their professional communities. *Educational Evaluation and Policy Analysis, 23*(2),
   145–170.

Coburn, C. E. (2006). Framing the problem of reading instruction: Using frame analysis to
   uncover the microprocesses of policy implementation. *American Educational Research
   Journal, 43*(3), 343–349.

Coburn, C. E., & Penuel, W. R. (2016). Research–practice partnerships in education: Outcomes,
   dynamics, and open questions. *Educational Researcher, 45*(1), 48–54.

Coburn, C. E., & Russell, J. L. (2008). District policy and teachers' social networks. *Educational
   Evaluation and Policy Analysis, 30*(3), 203–235. https://doi.org/10.3102/0162373708321829

Coburn, C. E., & Talbert, J. E. (2006). Conceptions of evidence use in school districts: Mapping
   the terrain. *American Journal of Education, 112*(4), 469–495.

Coburn, C. E., & Woulfin, S. L. (2012). Reading coaches and the relationship between policy
   and practice. *Reading Research Quarterly, 47*(1), 5–30.

Costa, A. L., & Garmston, R. J. (2015). *Cognitive coaching: Developing self-directed leaders and learners.* Rowman & Littlefield.

Cotto Jr, R., & Woulfin, S. (2021). Choice with (out) equity? Family decisions of child return to
   urban schools in pandemic. *Journal of Family Diversity in Education, 4*(1), 42–63.

Cox, E., Bachkirova, T., & Clutterbuck, D. A. (Eds.). (2014). *The complete handbook of coaching.*
   Sage.

Cuban, L. (1990). Reforming again, again, and again. *Educational Researcher, 19*(1), 3–13.

Deming, W. E. (1982). *Out of the crisis.* MIT Press.

Desimone, L. M., Porter, A. C., Garet, M. S., Yoon, K. S., & Birman, B. F. (2002). Effects of
   professional development on teachers' instruction: Results from a three-year longitudinal
   study. *Educational Evaluation and Policy Analysis, 24*(2), 81–112.

Deussen, T., Coskie, T., Robinson, L., & Autio, E. (2007). *"Coach" can mean many things: Five
   categories of literacy coaches in Reading First* (Issues & Answers Report). U.S. Department of
   Education, Institute of Education Sciences, National Center for Education Evaluation and
   Regional Assistance, Regional Educational Laboratory Northwest.

Diem, S., & Welton, A. D. (2020). *Anti-racist educational leadership and policy: Addressing racism in
   public education.* Routledge.

Dole, J. A. (2004). The changing role of the reading specialist in school reform. *The Reading
   Teacher, 57*(5), 462–471.

Domina, T., Lewis, R., Agarwal, P., & Hanselman, P. (2015). Professional sense-makers: Instructional specialists in contemporary schooling. *Educational Researcher, 44*(6), 359–364.
   https://doi.org/10.3102/0013189X15601644

DuFour, R. (2004). What is a "professional learning community"? *Educational Leadership, 61*(8),
   6–11.

DuFour, R., & Eaker, R. (1998). *Professional learning communities at work: Best practices for enhancing student achievement.* Solution Tree Press.

Earley, P. C., Connolly, T., & Ekegren, G. (1989). Goals, strategy development, and task performance: Some limits on the efficacy of goal setting. *Journal of Applied Psychology, 74*(1),
   24–33.

Eberhardt, J. L. (2020). Biased: Uncovering the hidden prejudice that shapes what we see,
   think, and do. Penguin.

Edmondson, A., & Verdin, P. (2017, November 13). Your strategy should be a hypothesis you constantly adjust. Retrieved May 26, 2020, from https://hbr.org/2017/11
   /your-strategy-should-be-a-hypothesis-you-constantly-adjust

El-Bawab, N. (2022). How to reverse the teacher crisis exacerbated by the pandemic.
   Retrieved May 1, 2022, from https://abcnews.go.com/US/reverse-teacher-crisis
   -exacerbated-pandemic-experts/story?id=83792346

Elfers, A. M., & Stritikus, T. (2014). How school and district leaders support classroom teachers'
   work with English language learners. *Educational Administration Quarterly, 50*(2), 305–344.

Evered, R. D., & Selman, J. C. (1989). Coaching and the art of management. *Organizational
   Dynamics, 18*(2), 16–32.

Farrell, C. C. (2015). Designing school systems to encourage data use and instructional improvement: A comparison of school districts and charter management organizations. *Educational
   Administration Quarterly, 51*(3), 438–471. https://doi.org/10.1177/0013161X14539806

Gabriel, R., & Woulfin, S. (2017). Making teacher evaluation work. Heinemann Press.

Galey-Horn, S., & Woulfin, S. L. (2021). Muddy waters: The micropolitics of instructional coaches' work in evaluation. *American Journal of Education, 127*(3), 441–470.

Garet, M. S., Porter, A. C., Desimone, L., Birman, B. F., & Yoon, K. S. (2001). What makes professional development effective? Results from a national sample of teachers. *American Educational Research Journal, 38*(4), 915–945.

Gawande, A. (2011). Personal best. *The New Yorker*.

Gay, G. (2018). Culturally responsive teaching: Theory, research, and practice. Teachers College Press.

Gibbons, L. K., & Cobb, P. (2016). Content-focused coaching: Five key practices. *The Elementary School Journal, 117*(2), 237–260.

Gibbons, L. K., & Cobb, P. (2017). Focusing on teacher learning opportunities to identify potentially productive coaching activities. *Journal of Teacher Education, 68*(4), 411–425. https://doi.org/10.1177/0022487117702579

Gibbons, L. K., Kazemi, E., & Lewis, R. M. (2017). Developing collective capacity to improve mathematics instruction: Coaching as a lever for school-wide improvement. *The Journal of Mathematical Behavior, 46*, 231–250. https://doi.org/10.1016/j.jmathb.2016.12.002

Goldhaber, D., Kane, T. J., McEachin, A., Morton, E., Patterson, T., & Staiger, D. O. (2022). *The consequences of remote and hybrid instruction during the pandemic* (No. w30010). National Bureau of Economic Research.

Goldring, E. B., Grissom, J. A., Rubin, M., Rogers, L. K., Neel, M., & Clark, M. A. (2018). *A new role emerges for principal supervisors: Evidence from six districts in the principal supervisor initiative*. Mathematica Policy Research, Inc.

Haager, D., Dhar, R., Moulton, M., & McMillian, S. (2008). The California reading first year 6 evaluation report. *Morgan Hill, CA: Educational Data Systems*.

Hallinger, P. (2005). Instructional leadership and the school principal: A passing fancy that refuses to fade away. *Leadership and Policy in Schools, 4*(3), 221–239. https://doi.org/10.1080/15700760500244793

Handsman, E., Farrell, C., & Coburn, C. (2022). Solving for X: Constructing algebra and algebra policy during a time of change. *Sociology of Education*, https://doi.org/00380407221087479

Hattie, J., & Clarke, S. (2018). *Visible learning: Feedback*. Routledge.

Heifetz, R. A., & Laurie, D. L. (1997). The work of leadership. *Harvard Business Review, 75*, 124–134.

Herd, P., & Moynihan, D. P. (2019). *Administrative burden: Policymaking by other means*. Russell Sage Foundation.

Hochberg, E. D., & Desimone, L. M. (2010). Professional development in the accountability context: Building capacity to achieve standards. *Educational Psychologist, 45*(2), 89–106.

Honig, M. I., & Rainey, L. (2020). *Supervising principals for instructional leadership: A teaching and learning approach*. Harvard Education Press.

Horsford, S. D., Scott, J. T., & Anderson, G. L. (2018). *The politics of education policy in an era of inequality: Possibilities for democratic schooling*. Routledge. https://www.nationalequityproject.org/frameworks/lens-of-systemic-oppression

Ippolito, J., Swan Dagen, A., & Bean, R. M. (2021). Elementary literacy coaching in 2021: What we know and what we wonder. *The Reading Teacher, 75*(2), 179–187.

Irby, D. J. (2021). *Stuck improving: Racial equity and school leadership. Race and education series*. Harvard Education Press.

Irby, D. J., Green, T., & Ishimaru, A. M. (2022). PK–12 district leadership for equity: An exploration of director role configurations and vulnerabilities. *American Journal of Education, 128*(3), 417–453.

Ivancevich, J. M., & McMahon, J. T. (1982). The effects of goal setting, external feedback, and self-generated feedback on outcome variables: A field experiment. *Academy of Management Journal, 25*(2), 359–372.

Jackson, C. K. (2020). *Does school spending matter? The new literature on an old question*. American Psychological Association.

Joyce, B. R., & Showers, B. (1981). Transfer of training: The contribution of "coaching." *Journal of Education, 163*(2), 163–172.

Kahneman, D. (2011). *Thinking, fast and slow*. Macmillan.

Kane, B. D., & Rosenquist, B. (2019). Relationships between instructional coaches' time use and district- and school-level policies and expectations. *American Educational Research Journal, 56*(5), 1718–1768.

Kendi, I. (2019). *How to be an antiracist.* One World.

Kersten, J., &. Pardo, L. (2007). Finessing and hybridizing: Innovative literacy practices in Reading First classrooms. *The Reading Teacher, 61*(2), 146–154.

Khalifa, M. A., Gooden, M. A., & Davis, J. E. (2016). Culturally responsive school leadership: A synthesis of the literature. *Review of Educational Research, 86*(4), 1272–1311.

Kluger, A. N., & DeNisi, A. (1996). The effects of feedback interventions on performance: A historical review, a meta-analysis, and a preliminary feedback intervention theory. *Psychological Bulletin, 119*(2), 254.

Knight, D. S. (2012). Assessing the cost of instructional coaching. *Journal of Education Finance, 38*(1), 52–80.

Kozlowski, S. W., & Ilgen, D. R. (2006). Enhancing the effectiveness of work groups and teams. *Psychological Science in the Public Interest, 7*(3), 77–124.

Kraft, M. A., Blazar, D., & Hogan, D. (2018). The effect of teacher coaching on instruction and achievement: A meta-analysis of the causal evidence. *Review of Educational Research.*

Ladson-Billings, G. (1995). Toward a theory of culturally relevant pedagogy. *American Educational Research Journal, 32*(3), 465–491.

Ladson-Billings, G. (2021). I'm here for the hard re-set: Post pandemic pedagogy to preserve our culture. *Equity & Excellence in Education, 54*(1), 68–78.

Lamb, A. J., & Weiner, J. M. (2021). Technology as infrastructure for change: District leader understandings of 1:1 educational technology initiatives and educational change. *Journal of Educational Administration, 59*(3). https://www.emerald.com/insight/content/doi/10.1108/JEA-10-2020-0220/full/html

Langley, G. J., Moen, R. D., Nolan, K. M., Nolan, T. W., Norman, C. L., & Provost, L. P. (2009). *The improvement guide: A practical approach to enhancing organizational performance.* John Wiley & Sons.

Lewis, A. E., & Diamond, J. B. (2015). *Despite the best intentions: How racial inequality thrives in good schools.* Oxford.

Little, J. W. (1982). Norms of collegiality and experimentation: Workplace conditions of school success. *American Educational Research Journal, 19*(3), 325–340.

Lochmiller, C. R. (2014). Leadership coaching in an induction program for novice principals: A 3-year study. *Journal of Research on Leadership Education, 9*(1), 59–84.

Lopez, B. (2022). It's Not Just COVID-19. https://www.keranews.org/texas-news/2022-07-25/its-not-just-covid-19-why-texas-faces-a-teacher-shortage

Lortie, D. C. (2002). *Schoolteacher.* University of Chicago Press.

Mangin, M. M. (2009). Literacy coach role implementation: How district context influences reform efforts. *Educational Administration Quarterly, 45*(5), 759–792. https://doi.org/10.1177/0013161x09347731

Mangin, M. M., & Dunsmore, K. (2015). How the framing of instructional coaching as a lever for systemic or individual reform influences the enactment of coaching. *Educational Administration Quarterly, 51*(2), 179–213. https://doi.org/10.1177/0013161X14522814

Marsh, J. A., Sloan McCombs, J., & Martorell, F. (2010). How instructional coaches support data-driven decision making: Policy implementation and effects in Florida middle schools. *Educational Policy, 24*(6), 872–907.

Matsumura, L. C., Garnier, H. E., & Resnick, L. B. (2010). Implementing literacy coaching: The role of school social resources. *Educational Evaluation and Policy Analysis, 32*(2), 249–272. https://doi.org/10.3102/0162373710363743

Matsumura, L. C., Garnier, H. E., & Spybrook, J. (2013). Literacy coaching to improve student reading achievement: A multi-level mediation model. *Learning and Instruction, 25*, 35–48. https://doi.org/10.1016/j.learninstruc.2012.11.001

Mehta, J., Yurkofsky, M., & Frumin, K. (2022). Linking continuous improvement and adaptive leadership. *Educational Leadership, 79*(6), 36–41.

Munson, J., & Saclarides, E. S. (2022). Getting a foot in the door: Examining content-focused coaches' strategies for gaining access to classrooms. *The Elementary School Journal, 123*(1).

Noonan, J., & Bristol, T. J. (2020). "Taking care of your own": Parochialism, pride of place, and the drive to diversify teaching. *AERA Open, 6*(4), https://doi.org/2332858420964433

Orange, T., Isken, J. A., Green, A., Parachini, N., & Francois, A. (2019). Coaching for equity. *The Learning Professional, 40*(6), 45–49.

Penuel, W. R., Fishman, B. J., Yamaguchi, R., & Gallagher, L. P. (2007). What makes professional development effective? Strategies that foster curriculum implementation. *American Educational Research Journal, 44*(4), 921–958.

Petersen, P. B. (1999). Total quality management and the Deming approach to quality management. *Journal of Management History (Archive), 5*(8), 468–488. https://doi.org/10.1108/13552529910290520

Peurach, D. J., Cohen, D. K., Yurkofsky, M. M., & Spillane, J. P. (2019). From mass schooling to education systems: Changing patterns in the organization and management of instruction. *Review of Research in Education, 43*(1), 32–67.

Pressley, T., Ha, C., & Learn, E. (2021). Teacher stress and anxiety during COVID-19: An empirical study. *School Psychology, 36*(5), 367.

Ray, V. (2022). *On critical race theory: Why it matters and why you should care.* Random House.

Rigby, J. G. (2014). Three logics of instructional leadership. *Educational Administration Quarterly, 50*(4), 610–644. https://doi.org/10.1177/0013161X13509379

Roegman, R., Allen, D., Leverett, L., Thompson, S., & Hatch, T. (2019). *Equity visits: A new approach to supporting equity-focused school and district leadership.* Corwin.

Rosenzweig, S. (1936). Some implicit common factors in diverse methods of psychotherapy. *American Journal of Orthopsychiatry, 6*(3), 412–415.

Ross, L., & Nisbett, R. E. (2011). *The person and the situation: Perspectives of social psychology.* Pinter & Martin Publishers.

Rowan, B. (2002). The ecology of school improvement: Notes on the school improvement industry in the United States. *Journal of Educational Change, 3*(3), 283–314.

Rowan, B., & Correnti, R. (2009). Studying reading instruction with teacher logs: Lessons from the study of instructional improvement. *Educational Researcher, 38*(2), 120–131.

Russell, J. L., Correnti, R., Stein, M. K., Thomas, A., Bill, V., & Speranzo, L. (2020). Mathematics coaching for conceptual understanding: Promising evidence regarding the Tennessee math coaching model. *Educational Evaluation and Policy Analysis, 42*(3), 439–466.

Safir, S. & Dugan, J. (2021). *Street data: The next generation model for equity, pedagogy, and school transformation.* Corwin.

Saltzman, A. (2016). *The power of principal supervisors: How two districts are remaking an old role. Stories from the field.* Wallace Foundation.

Seashore, C. N., Whitfield Seashore, E., & Weinberg, G. (1992). *What did you say? The art of giving and receiving feedback.* Douglas Charles Press.

Seijts, G. H., Latham, G. P., Tasa, K., & Latham, B. W. (2004). Goal setting and goal orientation: An integration of two different yet related literatures. *Academy of Management Journal, 47*(2), 227–239.

Sensoy, Ö. & DiAngelo, R. (2017). *Is everyone really equal? An introduction to key concepts in social justice education.* Teachers College Press.

Shewhart, W. A. (1931). *Economic control of quality of manufactured product.* Macmillan.

Shirrell, M., & Spillane, J. P. (2020). Opening the door: Physical infrastructure, school leaders' work-related social interactions, and sustainable educational improvement. *Teaching and Teacher Education, 88*, Article 102846.

Singleton, G. E. (2014). *Courageous conversations about race: A field guide for achieving equity in schools.* Corwin Press.

Smith, M. S., & O'Day, J. (1990). Systemic school reform. *Journal of Education Policy, 5*(5), 233–267. https://doi.org/10.1080/02680939008549074

Spillane, J. P., Reiser, B. J., & Reimer, T. (2002). Policy implementation and cognition: Reframing and refocusing implementation research. *Review of Educational Research, 72*(3), 387–431.

Steinberg, M. P., & Donaldson, M. L. (2016). The new educational accountability: Understanding the landscape of teacher evaluation in the post-NCLB era. *Education Finance and Policy, 11*(3), 340–359. https://doi.org/10.1162/EDFP_a_00186

Stelitano, L., Doan, S., Woo, A., Diliberti, M., Kaufman, J. H., & Henry, D. (2020). The digital divide and COVID-19: Teachers' perceptions of inequities in students' Internet access and participation in remote learning. Data Note: Insights from the American Educator Panels. Research Report. RR-A134-3. *Rand Corporation.*

Stevenson, I. (2017). What a question can accomplish. *The Learning Professional, 38*(3), 32.

Stevenson, I., & Weiner, J. M. (2020). *The strategy playbook for educational leaders: Principles and processes.* Routledge.

Stevenson, I., & Lemons, R. W., (2021). Improvement routines: Research by and for practitioners. *Phi Delta Kappan, 102*(7).

Thorson, G. R., & Gearhart, S. M. (2019). Do enhanced funding policies targeting students in poverty close achievement gaps? Evidence from the American states, 1996–2015. *Poverty & Public Policy, 11*(3), 205–221.

Trujillo, T. M. (2013). The politics of district instructional policy formation: Compromising equity and rigor. *Educational Policy, 27*(3), 531–559. https://doi.org/10.1177/0895904812454000

Trujillo, T. M., & Woulfin, S. L. (2014). Equity-oriented reform amid standards-based accountability: A qualitative comparative analysis of an intermediary's instructional practices. *American Educational Research Journal, 51*(2), 253–293.

Tschannen-Moran, B. & Tschannen-Moran, M. (2010). *Evocative coaching: Transforming schools one conversation at a time.* Jossey-Bass.

Tschannen-Moran, M. (2004). *Trust matters: Leadership for successful schools.* Jossey-Bass.

Tyack, D., & Cuban, L. (1995). *Tinkering toward utopia.* Harvard University Press.

Weiner, J., & Woulfin, S. L. (2018). Sailing across the divide: Challenges to the transfer of teacher leadership. *Journal of Research on Leadership Education,* https://doi.org/1942775118766319

Welton, A. D., Owens, D. R., & Zamani-Gallaher, E. M. (2018). Anti-racist change: A conceptual framework for educational institutions to take systemic action. *Teachers College Record, 120*(14), 1–22.

Wenger, E. (1998). Communities of practice: Learning as a social system. *Systems Thinker, 9*(5), 2–3.

Wenner, J. A., & Campbell, T. (2017). The theoretical and empirical basis of teacher leadership: A review of the literature. *Review of Educational Research, 87*(1), 134–171.

Woulfin, S., & Gabriel, R. E. (2020). Interconnected infrastructure for improving reading instruction. *Reading Research Quarterly, 55,* S109–S117.

Woulfin, S. L. (2015). Catalysts of change: An examination of coaches' leadership practices in framing a reading reform (2015). *Journal of School Leadership, 25*(3), 526–557.

Woulfin, S. L. (2016). Duet or duel? A portrait of two logics of reading instruction in an urban school district. *American Journal of Education, 122*(3), 337–365.

Woulfin, S. L. (2017). Coach professional development in the urban emergent context. *Urban Education, 55*(10), https://doi.org/0042085917714513

Woulfin, S. L. (2018). Mediating instructional reform: An examination of the relationship between district policy and instructional coaching. *AERA Open, 4*(3), https://doi.org/2332858418792278

Woulfin, S. L. (2020). Crystallizing coaching: An examination of the institutionalization of instructional coaching in three educational systems. *Teachers College Record, 122*(10).

Woulfin, S. L., & Allen, C. (2022). The institution of schooling. *The Foundational Handbook on Improvement Research in Education, 67.*

Woulfin, S. L., Donaldson, M. L., & Gonzales, R. (2016). District leaders' framing of educator evaluation policy. *Educational Administration Quarterly, 52*(1), 110–143.

Woulfin, S. L., & Rigby, J. G. (2017). Coaching for coherence: How instructional coaches lead change in the evaluation era. *Educational Researcher, 46*(6), 323–328.

Yeager, D. S., Purdie-Vaughns, V., Garcia, J., Apfel, N., Brzustoski, P., Master, A., . . . & Cohen, G. L. (2014). Breaking the cycle of mistrust: Wise interventions to provide critical feedback across the racial divide. *Journal of Experimental Psychology: General, 143*(2), 804.

Yurkofsky, M. (2022). From compliance to improvement: How school leaders make sense of institutional and technical demands when implementing a continuous improvement process. *Educational Administration Quarterly, 58*(2), 300–346.

Yurkofsky, M. M., Peterson, A. J., Mehta, J. D., Horwitz-Willis, R., & Frumin, K. M. (2020). Research on continuous improvement: Exploring the complexities of managing educational change. *Review of Research in Education, 44*(1), 403–433.

Index

About the Authors

Sarah L. Woulfin is an associate professor of educational leadership and policy at the University of Texas at Austin. Sarah uses organizational theory and qualitative methods to study the relationship between policy, leaders' work, and equitable instructional improvement. Sarah has studied the structures and practices of coaching across multiple states and district contexts. She has also engaged in partnership research on professional learning systems. These scholarly efforts have been supported by the Spencer Foundation and other organizations. Her research has been published in the *American Journal of Education, AERA Open, Educational Administration Quarterly, Urban Education*, and other outlets. Sarah has had the privilege of serving as an instructor for current and aspiring district and school leaders in Texas and Connecticut on instructional leadership, systemic reform, and policy implementation. Sarah earned her PhD in Education from the University of California–Berkeley. As a former Reading First reading coach and elementary school teacher, Sarah is dedicated to raising the quality of instruction for all students across all schools and improving working conditions for all teachers and leaders in our educational system.

Isobel Stevenson has over 30 years' experience in education, as a teacher, school principal, central office leader, consultant, and coach. Isobel holds an undergraduate degree from Oxford University, a master's in special education from the University of Texas at Austin, where she also obtained her principal's license. She served on the AP Committee of the College Board for AP Geography and was a consultant for *National Geographic*. Isobel has taught in three different principal preparation programs. She has a PhD in human and organizational systems from Fielding Graduate University and is a professional certified coach. Isobel's work currently includes equity and leadership coaching, strategic planning, and supporting instructional improvement. Isobel is the co-author of *The Strategy Playbook for Educational Leaders* (2020), and several articles on leadership and coaching. Isobel also writes a newsletter for educational leaders and coaches, *The Coaching Letter*.

Over the last 30 years, **Kerry Lord** has enjoyed an exciting career as a public educator. Kerry is the project manager for the annual Equity Institute, works with district leaders to address systemic inequities, coaches and mentors school leaders, and facilitates communities of practice designed to support school leaders. As an elementary teacher in San Francisco, Kerry worked with the Exploratorium Science Museum and the San Francisco Modern Art Museum to incorporate art and science inquiry into the school curriculum. During her 10 years in the Bay Area, Kerry taught elementary and middle school. As a school leader in Denver, Kerry served as a principal at the elementary level for 10 years, and then became the executive director at a K–12 Expeditionary Learning public school of choice. In 2009, Kerry was recognized by the Commissioner of Education for her school's outstanding student growth. Kerry served as an instructor for the Residency Program for School Leaders where she served as a leadership coach and seminar facilitator. Kerry holds a bachelor's degree from the University of Colorado and a master's in education from San Francisco State University.